D0374771

TO MY PARENTS, MR. AND MRS. HAN-PO CHUNG
Ling Chung

FOR CAROL
Kenneth Rexroth

WOMEN POETS
OF
CHINA

Translated and Edited by

KENNETH REXROTH
AND LING CHUNG

A NEW DIRECTIONS BOOK

Copyright © 1972 by Kenneth Rexroth and Ling Chung

All rights reserved. Except for brief passages quoted in a newspaper, magazine, radio or television review, no part of this book
may be reproduced in any form or by any means, electronic or
mechanical, including photocopying and recording, or by any
information storage and retrieval system, without permission in
writing from the Publisher.

The decorative calligraphy was written by Kao T'ai

Formerly published by The Seabury Press as *The Orchid Boat*.
Manufactured in the United States of America. New Directions books are printed on acid-free paper. First published as
New Directions Paperbook 528 in 1982. Published simultane-
ously in Canada by Penguin Books Canada Limited

Library of Congress Cataloging in Publication Data

Orchid boat.
   Women poets of China.
   (A New Directions Book)
   Previously published as: The Orchid boat.
1972.
   "New Directions paperbook 528."
   Bibliography: p. 148
   1. Chinese poetry—Translations into English.
2. English poetry—Translations from Chinese.
3. Chinese poetry—Women authors—I. Rexroth,
Kenneth, 1905–1982   II. Chung, Ling, 1945–
III. Title.
PL2658.E307   1982   895.1′1′00809287   81-18698
ISBN 0-8112-0821-4 (pbk.)   AACR2

New Directions Books are published for James Laughlin
by New Directions Publishing Corporation,
80 Eighth Avenue, New York 10011

EIGHTH PRINTING

CONTENTS

Lady Ho

(circa 300 B.C.)

A SONG OF MAGPIES

There are magpies on the South hill.
You set your net on the North hill.
The magpies soar free.
What good is your net?

When a pair of magpies fly together
They do not envy the pair of phoenixes.
My lord I am a common person—
I do not envy the Duke of Sung.

Chuo Wên-chün

(B.C. 2nd Century)

卓
文
君

A SONG OF WHITE HAIR

My love, like my hair, is pure,
Frosty white like the snow on the mountain
Bright and white like the moon amid the clouds.
But I have discovered
You are of a double mind.
We have come to the breaking point.
Today we pledged each other
In a goblet of wine.
Tomorrow I will walk alone
Beside the moat,
And watch the cold water
Flow East and West,
Lonely, mournful
In the bitter weather.
Why should marriage bring only tears?
All I wanted was a man
With a single heart,
And we would stay together
As our hair turned white,
Not somebody always after wriggling fish
With his big bamboo rod.
The integrity of a loyal man
Is beyond the value of money.

Pan Chieh-yü

(B.C. 1st Century)

A SONG OF GRIEF

I took a piece of the fine cloth of Ch'i,
White silk glowing and pure like frosted snow,
And made you a doubled fan of union and joy,
As flawlessly round as the bright moon.
It comes and goes in my Lord's sleeves.
You can wave it and start a cooling breeze.
But I am always afraid that when Autumn comes,
And the cold blasts drive away the heat,
You will store it away in a bamboo case,
And your love of it will stop midway.

Ts'ai Yen

(circa 200)

蔡
琰

FROM 18 VERSES SUNG
TO A TATAR REED WHISTLE

I

I was born in a time of peace,
But later the mandate of Heaven
Was withdrawn from the Han Dynasty.

Heaven was pitiless.
It sent down confusion and separation.
Earth was pitiless.
It brought me to birth in such a time.
War was everywhere. Every road was dangerous.
Soldiers and civilians everywhere
Fleeing death and suffering.
Smoke and dust clouds obscured the land
Overrun by the ruthless Tatar bands.
Our people lost their will power and integrity.
I can never learn the ways of the barbarians.
I am daily subject to violence and insult.
I sing one stanza to my lute and a Tatar horn.
But no one knows my agony and grief.

II

A Tatar chief forced me to become his wife,
And took me far away to Heaven's edge.
Ten thousand clouds and mountains
Bar my road home,
And whirlwinds of dust and sand
Blow for a thousand miles.
Men here are as savage as giant vipers,
And strut about in armor, snapping their bows.
As I sing the second stanza I almost break the
    lutestrings.
Will broken, heart broken, I sing to myself.

VII

The sun sets. The wind moans.
The noise of the Tatar camp rises all around me.
The sorrow of my heart is beyond expression,
But who could I tell it to anyway?
Far across the desert plains,
The beacon fires of the Tatar garrisons
Gleam for ten thousand miles.
It is the custom here to kill the old and weak
And adore the young and vigorous.
They wander seeking new pasture,
And camp for a while behind earth walls.
Cattle and sheep cover the prairie,
Swarming like bees or ants.
When the grass and water are used up,
They mount their horses and drive on their cattle.
The seventh stanza sings of my wandering.
How I hate to live this way!

XI

I have no desire to live, but I am afraid of death.
I cannot kill my body, for my heart still has hope
That I can live long enough
To obtain one and only desire—
That someday I can see again
The mulberry and catalpa trees of home.
If i had consented to death,
My bones would have been buried long ago.
Days and months pile up in the Tatar camp.
My Tatar husband loved me. I bore him two sons.
I reared and nurtured them unashamed,
Sorry only that they grew up in a desert outpost.
The eleventh stanza—sorrow for my sons
At the first notes pierces my heart's core.

XIII

I never believed that in my broken life
The day would come when
Suddenly I could return home.
I embrace and caress my Tatar sons.
Tears wet our clothes.
An envoy from the Han Court
Has come to bring me back,
With four stallions that can run without stopping.
Who can measure the grief of my sons?
They thought I would live and die with them.
Now it is I who must depart.
Sorrow for my boys dims the sun for me.
If we had wings we could fly away together.
I cannot move my feet,
For each step is a step away from them.
My soul is overwhelmed.
As their figures vanish in the distance
Only my love remains.
The thirteenth stanza—
I pick the strings rapidly
But the melody is sad.
No one can know
The sorrow which tears my bowels.

XVII

The seventeenth stanza. My heart aches, my tears fall.
Mountain passes rise before us, the way is hard.
Before I missed my homeland
So much my heart was disordered.
Now I think again and again, over and over,
Of the sons I have lost.
The yellow sagebrush of the border,
The bare branches and dry leaves,
Desert battlefields, white bones
Scarred with swords and arrows,
Wind, frost, piercing cold,
Cold springs and summers
Men and horses hungry and exhausted, worn out—
I will never know them again
Once I have entered Chang An.
I try to strangle my sobs
But my tears stream down my face.

TS'AI YEN

Mêng Chu

(3rd Century)

SPRING SONG

In the sunny Spring of March and April,
When water and grass are the same color,
I met a young man dallying along the road,
I'm sorry I didn't meet him earlier.

In the sunny Spring of March and April
When water and grass are the same color,
I reach up and pick the flowers from the vines.
Their perfume is like my lover's breath.

Four, now five years, I have expected you.
During this long wait my love
Has turned into sorrow.
I wish we could go away, back to some lonely place,
Where I could give my body
Completely to your embraces.

Tzu Yeh

(3rd–4th Centuries)

FIVE TZU YEH SONGS

I

I cannot sleep
For the blaze of the full moon.
I thought I heard here and there
A voice calling.
Hopelessly I answer "Yes."
To the empty air.

II

It is night again
I let down my silken hair
Over my shoulders
And open my thighs
Over my lover.
"Tell me, is there any part of me
That is not lovable?"

III

I had not fastened my sash over my gown,
When you asked me to look out the window.
If my skirt fluttered open,
Blame the Spring wind.

IV

The bare branches tremble
In the sudden breeze.
The twilight deepens.
My lover loves me,
And I am proud of my young beauty.

V

I am the North Pole
Steady for a thousand years.
Your sun-like heart
Goes East in the morning
And West in the evening.

TZU YEH

Anonymous

(5th Century)

ON THE SLOPE OF HUA MOUNTAIN

O Flowery Mountain slopes,
Now that my lover is dead
How can I live out my lonely life?

O my lover, if you still love me,
Open your sealed coffin for me,
And take me with you.

Why is it, with the world full of men
I am desolated, and long only for you?

I wish I were the ivy,
Climbing high in the pine tree,
And you were the moving clouds,
So we could see each other
As you pass by.

Su Hsiao-hsiao

(late 5th Century)

A SONG OF HSI-LING LAKE

I ride in a red painted carriage.
You pass me on a blue dappled horse.
Where shall we bind our hearts
In a love knot?
Along Hsi-ling Lake under the cypress trees.

Pao Ling-hui

(5th Century)

AFTER ONE OF THE
19 FAMOUS HAN POEMS

Slender bamboos grow by the window.
A tung tree overhangs the gate.
A dazzling beauty stands on the blue balcony.
It is cold and desolate in her high hall.
Her mind is pure as the Autumn frost.
Her jade face is more beautiful than Spring flowers.
She has nothing to regret about her life
Except that her Lord joined the army too early.
She is embarrassed to play the zither
In the moonlit night,
Or to paint her eyebrows
When the Spring wind blows.

Wu Tsê-t'ien

(624–705)

武
列
天

A LOVE SONG OF THE EMPRESS WU

I watch the red buds turn to green leaves.
My thoughts are many and tumultuous,
As troubled as the tossing branches,
All for thinking of you.
If you do not believe I have wept
Constantly since that time,
Open my wardrobe case
And examine my pomegranate flower dress.

Kuan P'an-p'an

(8th–9th Century)

MOURNING

In the cemetery on North Hill
Heavy mist envelops the pines and cypresses.
In Swallow Mansion
I sit quietly thinking of you.
Since you were buried
Your singers are scattered like dust.
And the perfume in their red sleeves
Has faded away for ten years now.

Li Yeh

(8th Century)

A GREETING TO LU HUNG-CHIEN
*Who came to visit me by the lake
in my illness*

Last time you left
The moon shone on heavy frosts.
Now today you have come through bitter fog
To visit me, still lying here ill.
When I try to speak, tears start.
You urge me to drink T'ao Chien's wine,
And I chant Hsieh Ling-yün's poems of welcome.
It is good to get drunk once in a while.
What else is there to do?

Yü Hsüan-chi

(mid 9th Century)

魚
玄
機

ADVICE TO A NEIGHBOR GIRL

Afraid of the sunlight,
You cover your face with your silk sleeves.
Tired out with Spring melancholy,
You neglect your makeup.
It is easier to get priceless jewels
Than to find a man with a true heart.
Why wet your pillow with secret tears?
Why hide your heartbreak in the flowers?
Go, seek a handsome famous man like Sung Yü.
Don't long for someone who will never come back.

LIVING IN THE SUMMER MOUNTAINS

I have moved to this home of Immortals.
Wild shrubs bloom everywhere.
In the front garden, trees
Spread their branches for clothes racks.
I sit on a mat and float wine cups
In the cool spring.
Beyond the window railing
A hidden path leads away
Into the dense bamboo grove.
In a gauze dress
I read among my disordered
Piles of books.
I take a leisurely ride
In the painted boat,
And chant poems to the moon.
I drift at ease, for I know
The soft wind will blow me home.

YÜ HSÜAN-CHI

ON A VISIT TO CH'UNG CHÊN TAOIST TEMPLE I SEE IN THE SOUTH HALL THE LIST OF SUCCESSFUL CANDIDATES IN THE IMPERIAL EXAMINATIONS

Cloud capped peaks fill the eyes
In the Spring sunshine.
Their names are written in beautiful characters
And posted in order of merit.
How I hate this silk dress
That conceals a poet.
I lift my head and read their names
In powerless envy.

YÜ HSÜAN-CHI

SENDING SPRING LOVE TO TZU-AN

The mountain path is steep
And the stone steps dangerous,
But I do not suffer from the hardships of the journey,
But from lovesickness.
The mountain torrent that comes
From far off melting ice
Is pure as your spiritual character.
When I see the snow on the distant mountains
I think of your jade-like beauty.
Do not listen to vulgar songs
Or drink too much Spring wine
Or play chess all night with idle guests.
Steady as a pine, not like a rolling stone,
My oath of love is forever.
I long for the days
When we will be together again
Like the birds that fly
With one wing in common.
I walk alone with my regrets, longing
All day long at the end of winter
For the time when we
Will be together again under the full moon.
What can I give you as a gift of separation —
Tears that glitter in the sun on a poem.

YÜ HSÜAN-CHI

Hsüeh T'ao

(768–831)

THE AUTUMN BROOK

It has turned crystal clear lately
And flows away like a ribbon of smoke
With a music like a ten stringed zither.
The sound penetrates to my pillow,
And turns my mind to past loves,
And won't let me sleep for melancholy.

AN OLD POEM TO YÜAN CHÊN

Each poem has its own pattern of tones.
I only know how to write
Delicate evanescent verse
About tranquil love making—
In the shadow of moonlit flowers,
Or on misty mornings under the weeping willows.
The Green Jade Concubine was kept hidden away.
But you should learn to write love poems
On red paper for the girls in the pleasure city.
I am getting old and can let myself go,
So I will teach you as though you were a schoolboy.

HSÜEH T'AO

Hsüeh Ch'iung

(9th Century?)

薛
瓊

A SONG OF CHIN MEN DISTRICT

Yellow birds flutter through the red maples
Black oxen rest in the green meadow
The palace of the Ch'u Kingdom stood here once,
A place of singing and dancing.
Now fine mists envelop the towers and terraces.

Han Ts'ui-p'in

(9th Century)

A POEM WRITTEN ON A FLOATING RED LEAF

How fast this water flows away!
Buried in the women's quarters,
The days pass in idleness.
Red leaf, I order you—
Go find someone
In the world of men.

Chang Wên-chi

(9th Century?)

張

文

姬

THE BAMBOO SHADED POOL

My lord contemplates a pool
Where the branches droop over the water,
And the jade green ripples,
Day after day, flow without end.

Chao Luan-luan

(8th Century?)

SLENDER FINGERS

Slender, delicate, soft jade,
Fresh peeled spring onions—
They are always hidden in emerald
Sleeves of perfumed silk.
Yesterday on the lute strings
All their nails were painted scarlet.

RED SANDALWOOD MOUTH

Small cherries sip delicately
At the edge of the wine cup.
Beautiful speech floats on jasmine perfume.
Like the mouth of the singer Fan Su,
The concubine of Po Chü-i,
The teeth are like white melon seeds,
And the lips like pomegranate blossoms.

CHAO LUAN-LUAN

WILLOW EYEBROWS

Sorrows play at the edge of these willow leaf curves.
They are often reflected, deep, deep,
In my water blossom inlaid mirror.
I am too pretty to bother with an eyebrow pencil.
Spring hills paint themselves
With their own personality.

CHAO LUAN-LUAN

CLOUD HAIRDRESS

My disordered perfumed clouds are still damp,
Iridescent as a blackbird's throat feathers,
Glossy as a cicada's wing.
I pin a gold phoenix by my ear.
After I have adorned myself,
My man smiles at me.

CHAO LUAN-LUAN

CREAMY BREASTS

Fragrant with powder, moist with perspiration,
They are the pegs of a jade inlaid harp.
Aroused by spring, they are soft as cream
Under the fertilizing mist.
After my bath my perfumed lover
Holds them and plays with them
And they are cool as peonies and purple grapes.

CHAO LUAN-LUAN

Lady Hua Jui

(10th Century)

THE EMPEROR ASKS WHY
MY HUSBAND SURRENDERED

My Lord raised a flag of surrender
Over the Emperor's city.
Buried deep in the women's quarters,
How can I understand
Why a hundred and forty thousand
Soldiers laid down their arms.
All I can say is—
There was not a man amongst them.

LIFE IN THE PALACE

I

The mansions of the concubines
Surround the Imperial Palace.
Gold chimes blend with phoenix mouth organs.
All through the moonlit night,
Under the blossoming trees by the lake,
There is always the sound of singing.

II

In silk gown and jade belt
I am graceful as a phoenix,
With silver pins behind my ear,
And a scarf about my hair.
When I hear in the front hall
An order for the emperor's horse,
I strike my horse whip,
And ride across the little red terrace.

III

In the early morning
Of the Spring day
The gardeners bring the flowers
From the royal gardens.
The pink buds are delicate,
As fresh tinted clouds.
Kneeling on the jade staircase,
They present them still wet with dew.
Immediately the emperor announces
They are to be given to the Palace women.

IV

At the first of the month
Money to buy flowers is given
To the several thousand waiting women
In all the palaces.
When my name is called
I am not there to answer.
I am lasciviously posturing
Before the emperor
As he lies in bed.

LADY HUA JUI

Ch'ien T'ao

(early 11th Century)

WRITTEN AT A PARTY
WHERE MY LORD GAVE AWAY
A THOUSAND BOLTS OF SILK

A bolt of silk for each clear toned song.
Still these beauties do not think it is enough.
Little do they know of a weaving girl,
Sitting cold by her window,
Endlessly throwing her shuttle to and fro.

Lady Wei

(late 11th–12th Centuries)

To the tune "The Bodhisattva's Barbaric Headdress"

The rays of the low sun,
Reflected on the stream,
Glow on the hills.
As shadows envelop the house and terrace,
The mandarin ducks fly to their roost.
On the opposite shore
Red almond blossoms
Stand out against the walls of the village.
Morning and evening I walk
Along the banks of the stream
Under the green willows.
Three years now I have watched
The willow cotton flying
And my man who is gone
Has not come back.

Li Ch'ing-chao

(1084–1151)

To the short tune "The Magnolias"

From a flower carrying pole
I bought a spray of Spring in bud,
All moist as if with tears,
Still holding the pink clouds of dawn
And traces of the morning dew.
Lest my lover should think
My face not as lovely as the flowers
I pin it slanting in my cloud like hair
And ask him to make a comparison.

To the tune "A Hilly Garden"

Spring has come to the women's quarters.
The grass turns green.
The red buds of the plum trees have cracked
But are not yet fully open.
Blue green clouds carve jade dragons.
The jade powder becomes fine dust.
I try to hold on to my morning dream,
But I am startled by the breaking cup of Spring.
Flower shadows lie heavy on the garden gate.
A pale moon is spread on the translucent curtain
In the beautiful orange twilight.
For two years, three times, I have missed
The Lord of Spring.
Now he is coming home,
And I will thoroughly enjoy this Spring.

LI CH'ING-CHAO

HAPPY AND TIPSY
To the tune "A Dream Song"

I remember in Hsi T'ing,
All the many times
We got lost in the sunset,
Happy with wine,
And could not find our way back
After our pleasure was fulfilled.
We turned the boat in the darkness.
By mistake we rowed into dense
Clusters of lotus blossoms,
And startled the gulls and egrets
From the sand bars.
They crowded into the air
And hastily flapped away
To the opposite shore.

LI CH'ING-CHAO

THE SORROW OF DEPARTURE
To the tune "Butterflies Love Flowers"

The warm rain and pure wind
For the first time have broken
And driven away the chill.
Moist as the willows,
Light as the plum blossoms,
My heart revives with the Spring.
But now there is no one to share with me
The joys of wine and poetry.
Tears streak my rouge.
My hairpins are too heavy.
I put on my new quilted robe
Sewn with gold thread
And throw myself against a pile of pillows,
Crushing my phoenix hairpins.
Alone, all I can embrace is my sorrow.
I know a good dream will not come.
So I stay up until past midnight
Trimming the lamp flower's smoking wick.

LI CH'ING-CHAO

SPRING ENDS
To the tune "Spring in Wu-ling"

The wind stops.
Nothing is left of Spring but fragrant dust.
Although it is late in the day,
I have been too exhausted to comb my hair.
Our furniture is just the same,
But he no longer exists.
I am unable to do anything at all,
Before I can speak my tears choke me.
I hear that Spring at Two Rivers
Is still beautiful.
I had hoped to take a boat there,
But I am afraid my little boat
Is too small to ever reach Two Rivers,
Laden with my heavy sorrow.

LI CH'ING-CHAO

To the tune "The Honor of a Fisherman"

The heavens join with the clouds.
The great waves merge with the fog.
The Milky Way appears
Turning overhead.
A thousand sails dance.
I am rapt away to the place of the Supreme,
And hear the words of Heaven,
Asking me where I am going.
I answer, "It is a long road, alas,
Far beyond the sunset."
I try to put it into verse
But my words amaze me.
The huge roc bird is flying
On a ninety thousand mile wind.
O wind, do not stop
Until my little boat has been blown
To the Immortal Islands
In the Eastern Sea.

LI CH'ING-CHAO

To the tune "Eternal Happiness"

The setting sun is molten gold.
The evening clouds form a jade disc.
Where is he?
The willows are soft in the thick mist.
A sad flute plays "Falling Plum Blossoms."
How many Springs have I known?
This Feast of Lights should be joyful.
The weather is calm and lovely.
But who can tell if it
Will be followed by wind and rain?
A friend sends her perfumed carriage
And high bred horses to fetch me.
I thank my old poetry and wine companion.
I remember the happy days in the lost capital.
We took our ease in the women's quarters.
The Feast of Lights was elaborately celebrated—
Golden jewelry, brocaded girdles,
New sashes, we competed
To see who was most smartly dressed.
Now I am withering away,
Wind blown hair, frosty temples.
I am embarrassed to go out this evening.
I prefer to stay beyond the curtains,
And listen to talk and laughter
I can no longer share.

LI CH'ING-CHAO

Anonymous

(Courtesan)

To the tune "I Paint My Lips Red"

After kicking on the swing,
Lasciviously, I get up and rouge my palms.
Thick dew on a frail flower,
Perspiration soaks my thin dress.
A new guest enters.
My stockings come down
And my hairpins fall out.
Embarrassed, I run away,
And lean flirtatiously against the door,
Tasting a green plum.

Anonymous Courtesan
Sometimes attributed to
LI CH'ING CHAO

Anonymous

(Courtesan)

八燕名代

To the tune "Picking Mulberries"

As evening comes
A sudden rain and wind
Washes away the blazing light.
I play the mouth organ for a while, and then
Lightly dress myself
Before the water-flower ornamented mirror.
In my transparent purple chemise
My white skin glows,
Fragrant, and smooth as snow.
I smile to my lover and say,
"Tonight within the gauze curtains of our bed
The pillows and mats will be cool."

Anonymous Courtesan
attributed to
LI CH'ING CHAO

Chu Shu-chên

(early 12th Century)

SPRING JOY

Drafty winds and fine rain
Make a chilly Spring.
I drink wine, remembering bygone happiness,
Under the pear blossoms,
Weeping with misery.
Through the scented grasses
And broken mists, we walked
Along the Southern bank of the river,
Tears of farewell
Blurring the distant mountains.
Last night I was fulfilled in a dream.
Speechless, we made love
In mist and clouds.
Alas, when I awoke
The old agony returned.
I tossed in my quilt
Angry at my own helplessness.
It is easier to see Heaven
Than to see you.

SPRING NIGHT
To the tune "Panning Gold"

My jade body, like my gold hairpins,
Is still as lovely as it was that evening
When for the first time,
You turned me away from the lamplight
And unfastened the belt
Of my embroidered skirt.
Now our quilts and pillows are cold,
And the incense of that evening has long faded.
Behind the closed doors of the deep courtyard
Spring is silent and lonely.
Flowers fall with the rain, all the long night.
Agony mingles with my dreams
And makes me still more helpless
And hopeless.

CHU SHU-CHÊN

PLUM BLOSSOMS

The snow dances and the frost flies.
Through the bamboo blinds I see vaguely
The sparse shadows of slanting plum branches.
Unexpectedly a cold perfume,
Borne with the sound of a Tatar flute,
Is blown to our bed curtains.
Enveloped in this puzzling scented wind,
Who can appreciate such a subtle joy?
I quickly get up
In my dishevelled cloud dark hair.
We taste the stamens
And adorn ourselves with the blossoms,
Frowning and smiling,
Still drowsy with wine.

CHU SHU-CHÊN

PLAYING ALL A SUMMER'S DAY
BY THE LAKE
To the tune "Clear Bright Joy"

It is sad that the mist and fog are gathering
But hold me for a while, still;
And let us go back hand in hand
Along the path by the lotus ponds.
Suddenly fine rain falls on the yellow plum orchard.
I forget my bashfulness,
And abandon myself to your arms in my thin dress.
Finally the unbearable moment
Comes when we have to part.
I go home, and idly
Stare into my toilet table mirror.

CHU SHU-CHÊN

Nieh Shêng-ch'iung

(11th Century?)

FAREWELL TO LI
To the tune "A Partridge Sky"

Jade turns dull, flowers wilt
Because you are leaving Phoenix City.
The willows are bright green
Below the terraced lotus pools.
I sing for you a farewell song—
"Sunlight in the Mountain Pass."
We ride side by side as far
As the fifth milestone.

I try to dream good dreams
But it is hard to do
For those who have known
Moments of love as we have.
Tears on my pillow,
Rain on the staircase,
Raindrops streak my window until morning.

T'ang Wan

(12th Century)

To the tune "The Phoenix Hairpin"

The world's love runs thin.
Human love turns evil.
Rain strips, in the yellow twilight,
The flowers from the branches.
The dawn wind will dry my tear stains.
I try to write down the trouble of my heart.
I can only speak obliquely, exhausted.
It is hard, hard,
We are each of us all alone.
Today is not yesterday.
My troubled mind sways
Like the rope of a swing.
A horn sounds in the cold depth of the night.
Afraid of people's questions,
I will swallow my tears
And pretend to be happy.
Deceit. Deceit. Deceit.

Sun Tao-hsüan

(12th Century)

To the tune "A Dream Song"

The shadows of the torn green
Plantain leaves toss in disorder.
Half of the full moon
Rises above the vermillion balcony.
The wind blows down from the emerald sky
A song like a string of pearls.
But the singer is invisible
Hidden behind her embroidered curtains.

Wang Ch'ing-hui

(13th Century)

王
清
惠

To the tune "The River Is Red"

Now the lotuses in the imperial lake
Must look entirely different from the old days.
I remember when I received the gracious
Rain and dew, in the Emperor's golden bed
In the jade palace, and my fame spread
Like orchid incense amongst the queens and
    concubines.
I blushed like a lotus blossom
Whenever I was summoned to my Lord's side.
Suddenly, one day, war drums on horseback
Came like thunder, tearing off the sky,
And all the glorious flowery days were gone forever.
Generals scattered like dragons and tigers.
Courtiers fled like clouds in the storm.
To whom can I tell
My everlasting sorrow for the dead?
I look out on the mountains and rivers of this fastness,
And my tears mingle with blood on my sleeves.
I wake in a posthouse from dreams of dust and dirt.
Fleeing in the dawn, our palace carts
Roll through the mountain pass
Under the setting moon.
I pray to Ch'ang-O,
The girl who fled for refuge to the moon,
And ask her to permit me
To follow her to safety.

Kuan Tao-shêng

(1262–1319)

MARRIED LOVE

You and I
Have so much love,
That it
Burns like a fire,
In which we bake a lump of clay
Molded into a figure of you
And a figure of me.
Then we take both of them,
And break them into pieces,
And mix the pieces with water,
And mold again a figure of you,
And a figure of me.
I am in your clay.
You are in my clay.
In life we share a single quilt.
In death we will share one coffin.

Anonymous

(Yüan Dynasty)

COURTESAN'S SONGS
To the tune "Red Embroidered Shoes"

I

I hold you tight in my jade white arms.
You loosen my dress and my cloud dark hair.
The tips of our tongues are cold with passion
And sweet in each other's mouths.
You whisper my name.
I whisper yours.
Frantically we kiss each other
Again and again, here and there.

II

It is hard, loving this way.
We don't dare play with one another.
All we can do is steal a few words
When nobody notices.
When there are people around
We exchange sidelong glances.
I saw your long heavy sigh.
It delighted my eyes.
But it tore my heart.

Chu Chung-hsien

(15th Century)

朱
仲
嫻

To the tune "A Branch of Bamboo"

There is a wine shop by the shore of West Lake.
Its banner waves high in the Spring breeze.
A passerby buys some wine and sings a song,
And tramples the fallen wild almond petals.

A still pond in the old age of Autumn—
The lotus flowers are all withered.
Two by two, girls of the South row their boats back,
And startle
A pair of mandarin ducks from their swim.
They fly away, flapping over
The white rushes on the opposite shore.

Anonymous

(16th Century)

八
無
然
名
氏

A SONG OF THE DICE

A piece of fossil ivory
Carved with faces and hearts—
Ever since it was marked
It has been thrown until today.

Huang O

(1498–1569)

To the tune "The Fall of a Little Wild Goose"

Once upon a time I was
Beautiful and seductive,
Wavering to and fro in
Our orchid scented bedroom.
You and me together tangled
In our incense filled gauze
Bed curtains. I trembled,
Held in your hands. You carried
Me in your heart wherever
You went. Suddenly
A bullet struck down the female
Mandarin duck. The music
Of the jade zither was forgotten.
The phoenixes were driven apart.

I sit alone in a room
Filled with Spring, and you are off,
Making love with someone else,
Happy as two fish in the water.

That insufferable little bitch
With her coy tricks!
She'd better not forget —
This old witch can still
Make a furious scene!

A FAREWELL TO
A SOUTHERN MELODY

The day will come when I will
Share once more the quilts
And pillows I am storing
Away. Once more I will shyly
Let you undress me and gently
Unlock my sealed jewel.
I can never describe the
Ten thousand beautiful sensual
Ways we will make love.

HUANG O

To the tune "A Floating Cloud
Crosses Enchanted Mountain"

Every morning I get up
Beautiful as the Goddess
Of Love in Enchanted Mountain.
Every night I go to bed
Seductive as Yang Kuei-fei,
The imperial concubine.
My slender waist and thighs
Are exhausted and weak
From a night of cloud dancing.
But my eyes are still lewd,
And my cheeks are flushed.
My old wet nurse combs
My cloud-like hair.
My lover, fragrant as incense,
Adjusts my jade hairpins, and
Draws on my silk stockings
Over my feet and legs
Perfumed with orchids;
And once again we fall over
Overwhelmed with passion.

HUANG O

To the tune "Soaring Clouds"

You held my lotus blossom
In your lips and played with the
Pistil. We took one piece of
Magic rhinoceros horn
And could not sleep all night long.
All night the cock's gorgeous crest
Stood erect. All night the bee
Clung trembling to the flower
Stamens. Oh my sweet perfumed
Jewel! I will allow only
My lord to possess my sacred
Lotus pond, and every night
You can make blossom in me
Flowers of fire.

HUANG O

To the tune "Red Embroidered Shoes"

If you don't know how, why pretend?
Maybe you can fool some girls,
But you can't fool Heaven.
I dreamed you'd play with the
Locust blossom under my green jacket,
Like a eunuch with a courtesan.
But lo and behold
All you can do is mumble.
You've made me all wet and slippery,
But no matter how hard you try
Nothing happens. So stop.
Go and make somebody else
Unsatisfied.

HUANG O

To the tune "Plucking a Cinnamon Branch"

My lord, you only want to
Torture me. Into whose courtyard
Has my heavenly flower fallen?
We played together under
The covers, held in each other's arms.
Now nothing is left but sighs
Of misery.
At last the brave general
Saved Ying Ying from the bandit.
Do not let this young phoenix
Be married to an old crow.
But you are at the far corner
Of the sea and of heaven.
They say even distant mountains
At last will meet one another.
But I am frightened and anxious
And cannot ease my burning heart.

HUANG O

Ma Hsiang-lan

(16th century)

WATERLILIES

The floss of the reed flowers
Is like flying snow.
The Autumn river turns cold.
A jade inlaid horizontal flute
Sounds above the noise of men.
The wild geese return
On the first Autumn gales.
Here and there waterlilies are still blooming.

After the heavy dew, it is hard
For the beauty to get up.
Her perfumed rouge
Is reflected in the Autumn water,
A slanting flowered branch in a mirror,
Beautiful as an evening cloud.

Shao Fei-fei

(17th Century)

A LETTER

I trim my lamp, and weeping write this letter,
Seal, and send it ten thousand miles,
To tell you how wretched I am
And beg you to free my body.
Dear mother, how much is left of my bride price?

Wang Wei

(17th Century)

SEEKING A MOORING

A leaf floats in e   ess space.
A cold wind tears the clouds.
The water flows westward.
The tide pushes upstream.
Beyond the moonlit reeds,
In village after village, I hear
The sound of fullers' mallets
Beating the wet clothing
In preparation for winter.
Everywhere crickets cry
In the autumn frost.
A traveller's thoughts in the night
Wander in a thousand miles of dreams.
The sound of a bell cannot disperse
The sorrows that come
In the fifth hour of night.
What place will I remember
From all this journey?
Only still bands of desolate mist
And a single fishing boat.

Ho Shuang-ch'ing

(18th Century)

To the tune "A Watered Silk Dress"

The hardest thing in the world
Is to reveal a hidden love.
I swallow my tears
But still they come.
I twist the faded flowers of my hands
And lean speechless against my screen.
When I look in the mirror
My wasted figure frightens me.
Not a springlike face.
Not an autumnal face.
Is this me? Shuang-ch'ing?

To the tune "Washing Silk in the Stream"

The warm rain falls unfeeling
Like scattered silk threads.
The farm boy puts a flower behind his ear
As he carries the new grain
From his little field to the threshing floor.
I got up early to water the field
But he was angry with me
For being too early.
I cooked millet for him
Over a smoky fire
But he was angry because it was too late.
My tender bottom is sore all day long.

HO SHUANG-CH'ING

Sun Yün-fêng

(1764–1814)

ON THE ROAD THROUGH CHANG-TE

On the last year's trip I enjoyed this place.
I am glad to come back here today.
The fish market is deep in blue shadows.
I can see the smoke for tea rising
From the thatched inn.
The sands of the river beaches
Merge with the white moon.
Along the shore the willows
Wait for their Spring green.
Lines of a poem run through my mind.
I order the carriage to stop for a while.

TRAVELLING IN THE MOUNTAINS

Travelling homesick with the West wind,
The dust of my cart rises to the evening clouds.
The last cicadas drone in the yellowing leaves.
In the sunset a man's shadow looms like a mountain.
One by one the birds go to roost.
I wander aimlessly and never go home.
I pause above a stream and envy the fisherman
Who sits there in solitude and leisure,
Thinking his own elegant thoughts.

SUN YÜN-FÊNG

STARTING AT DAWN

Under the waning moon
In the dawn —
A frosty bell.
My horse's hooves
Tramp through the yellow leaves.
As the sun rises
Not a human being is visible
Only the sound of a stream
Through the misty trees.

SUN YÜN-FÊNG

THE TRAIL UP WU GORGE

The trail climbs in zig-zags
High above spiralling whirlpools.
Swift waters break against sheer rocks.
On the evening breeze comes the sound
Of a boy playing his flute,
Riding home on the back of an ox.
The last drops of rain mingle
With the cloud of my horse's breath.
New grass grows on the ancient ramparts.
On the abandoned monuments
The old inscriptions are lost in time.
I am bound on a journey without end,
And can not bear the song of the cuckoo.

SUN YÜN-FÊNG

Wu Tsao

(19th Century)

To the tune "The Pain of Lovesickness"

Once again a yellow twilight
Fills my deep courtyard.
Once again I am writing
The same sad verses on beautiful paper.
Once again my autumn lamp
Burns with the same dreams.
Last night there were whistling winds and rain.
Again tonight there will be the same.
Drip, drop—it will go on until
The sky is bright again.
The sound of the rain is so mournful,
From now on I will plant
Fewer banana trees.
The cold crickets have come indoors
And cry under the staircase.
Outside the window others cry to come in.
Beyond the wall the same shrill cries
Over and over again.

FOR THE COURTESAN CH'ING LIN
To the tune "The Love of the Immortals"

On your slender body
Your jade and coral girdle ornaments chime
Like those of a celestial companion
Come from the Green Jade City of Heaven.
One smile from you when we meet,
And I become speechless and forget every word.
For too long you have gathered flowers,
And leaned against the bamboos,
Your green sleeves growing cold,
In your deserted valley:
I can visualize you all alone,
A girl harboring her cryptic thoughts.

You glow like a perfumed lamp
In the gathering shadows.
We play wine games
And recite each other's poems.
Then you sing "Remembering South of the River"
With its heart breaking verses. Then
We paint each other's beautiful eyebrows.
I want to possess you completely—
Your jade body
And your promised heart.
It is Spring.
Vast mists cover the Five Lakes.
My dear, let me buy a red painted boat
And carry you away.

WU TSAO

To the tune "The Joy of
Peace and Brightness"

Bitter rain in my courtyard
In the decline of Autumn,
I only have vague poetic feelings
That I cannot bring together.
They diffuse into the dark clouds
And the red leaves.
After the yellow sunset
The cold moon rises
Out of the gloomy mist.
I will not let down the blinds
Of spotted bamboo from their silver hook.
Tonight my dreams will follow the wind,
Suffering the cold,
To the jasper tower of your beautiful flesh.

WU TSAO

To the tune "Flowers Along the Path through the Field"

I have closed the double doors.
In what corner of the heavens is she?
A horizontal flute
Beyond the red walls
Blown as gently as the breeze
Blows the willow floss.
In the lingering glow of the sunset
The roosting crows ignore my melancholy.
Once again I languidly get out of bed.
After I have burned incense,
I loiter on the jeweled staircase.
I regret the wasted years,
Sick, afraid of the cold, afraid of the heat,
While the beautiful days went by.
Suddenly it is the Autumn Feast of the Dead.
Constantly disturbed by the changing weather,
I lose track of the flowing light
That washes us away.
Who moved the tuning bridges
On my inlaid psaltery?
I realize—
Of the twenty five strings
Twenty one are gone.

WU TSAO

RETURNING FROM FLOWER LAW MOUNTAIN ON A WINTER DAY
To the tune "Washing Silk in the Stream"

All the way back I watch the mountains.
As the road twists the mountains turn.
As evening comes on, the mist
Turns to slanting rain
On the narrow planks across the cliffs,
And the reed flowers glow white in the twilight,
Blown by the sobbing wind.

The grave mounds of a thousand years
Are piled high.
How many broken tombstones?
How many buried human bones?
How many weeping mourners?
Snow flies into the red glowing fireplace.
The fireplace turns cold.
Millions of years of decline lie ahead of us
As destruction turns into ashes.

WU TSAO

IN THE HOME OF THE SCHOLAR WU SU-CHIANG FROM HSIN-AN, I SAW TWO PSALTERIES OF THE LATE SUNG GENERAL HSIEH FANG-TÊ

Half of our borders, rivers and mountains were gone,
With their Spring orioles and blossoms.
Your former career was only a painful memory.
You watched the melancholy moon set
Over an abandoned temple in the wilderness.
You could no longer see the beacon fires of Sung,
So you lived disguised as a fortune teller,
In a kiosk on a bridge, and no one knew you.
You who had a will of iron,
And held back the billowing flood of the world,
All by yourself in a besieged city.
You chanted Tu Fu's songs of homesickness,
You chose death to preserve your integrity.
At the end of the years of hiding
On these slopes amongst the tea bushes
Haunted by the cuckoos crying as if in pain,
You left behind two psalteries
Of tung wood and these ancient songs,
And went to death, a handful of yellow dust,
But deserving a royal grave.
Now as I play them I can imagine
Dragons dancing in the depths
And the moss on the shore burning red.

WU TSAO

To the tune "A Dream Song"

One swallow did not follow
The departed Spring
But hid in my embroidered curtains,
Gently, continuously chirping.
Do you want to live with me?
"Stay! Stay! Please!" he begs.
But I answer, "No."

WU TSAO

Yü Ch'ing-tsêng

(late 19th Century)

*To the tune "Intoxicated with
Shadows of Flowers"*

A brush of evening clouds.
The perfume of flowers in the darkness.
A harp melody
Accompanies the chanting of poetry.
Smoke rises from the incense clock's seal characters.
We lock the silk sliding doors,
And let down the curtains of the bed,
And whisper the words
We do not want others to hear.
The moonlight flows like water.
All the world is still.
My young lover can read my mind.
Laughing, we wash away my makeup,
And watch our love making in the mirror.

Ch'iu Chin

(1879?–1907)

A CALL TO ACTION

Without warning their nest
Has become dangerous to the swallows.
Our homeland, grown old, suffers
Under heavy burdens—
From the East the constant threat of invasion,
From the West, threats of devious plotting.
Scholars, throw away your brushes!
Secluded women, take up arms!
Only heroes can save us this time.
Together we can hold back
The flooding waves.

A LETTER TO LADY T'AO CH'IU
To the tune "Walking through the Sedges"

All alone with my shadow,
I whisper and murmur to it,
And write strange characters
In the air, like Yin Hao.
It is not sickness, nor wine,
Nor sorrow for those who are gone,
Like Li Ch'ing-chao, that causes
A whole city of anxiety
To rise in my heart.
There is no one here I can speak to
Who can understand me.
My hopes and visions are greater
Than those of the men around me,
But the chance of our survival is too narrow.
What good is the heart of a hero
Inside my dress?
My perilous fate moves according to plan.
I ask Heaven
Did the heroines of the past
Encounter envy like this?

CH'IU CHIN

Two poems to the tune
"The Narcissus by the River"

I

Lady T'ao Ch'ui-tse gave a farewell party in T'ao Jan
Pavilion. My woman friend Tzu-ying wrote couplets in
Great Cave calligraphy:

Like a young colt running past a crack in a wall,
The light and darkness of almost a year have gone by.
Wind sweeps the clouds from the sky.
We each go our separate ways.

I share her sadness and write a poem in answer.
I am going to Japan to study
And Tse-ying returns to the South.

II

We have drunk wine and discussed literature.
Our hearts have beat together
With the same emotions.
Softly we sing together the old song
"The Sunlight in the Pass."
The sorrow of parting will follow our horses' feet.
The melancholy of farewell
Surrounds the city like a river.
Iron strokes, silver curves, your couplets
Are limitless in their meanings.
Take care of yourself. We can have no confidence
That one day we will see each other again.
We stand on the bridge, hand in hand.
The river and the evening clouds stretch away for a
   thousand miles.

CH'IU CHIN

To the tune "The River Is Red"

How many wise men and heroes
Have survived the dust and dirt of the world?
How many beautiful women have been heroines?
There were the noble and famous women generals
Ch'in Liang-yü and Shen Yün-yin.
Though tears stained their dresses
Their hearts were full of blood.
The wild strokes of their swords
Whistled like dragons and sobbed with pain.

The perfume of freedom burns my mind
With grief for my country.
When will we ever be cleansed?
Comrades, I say to you,
Spare no effort, struggle unceasingly,
That at last peace may come to our people.
And jewelled dresses and deformed feet
Will be abandoned.
And one day, all under heaven
Will see beautiful free women,
Blooming like fields of flowers,
And bearing brilliant and noble human beings.

CH'IU CHIN

Ping Hsin

(1900–)

REMEMBERING

I tear off the calendar,
What day is today?
It is as though a cloud,
Black as a crow,
Swept across my eyes.
I want to be a woman of peace and a philosopher.
I forbid myself to think of him.
But I can think only of him.
I am just the kind of person I am.
I am not a woman of peace.
I am not qualified to be a philosopher.
I only know,
If a man loves me I love him;
If he dislikes me I dislike him.
A piece of land small as a leaf
Will be my home. I can never forget him.

FOR THE RECORD
(given to my little brother)

His right hand holds his slingshot,
His left a clay pellet.
He sits there, back against a pillar,
His legs straight, watching the sky
With his black eyes,
Stalking the crows that come
To steal the grapes from the arbor.
He intends to kill, but he cannot
Change his expresssion—filled with affection.
When I suddenly caught sight of him
From the window,
My eyes filled with tears.

PING HSIN

from MULTITUDINOUS STARS
AND SPRING WATERS

I

Sprays of frost flowers form
When the North wind blows gently.

II

Void only—
Take away your veil of stars
Let me worship
The splendor of your face.

III

These fragmented verses
Are only drops of spray
On the sea of knowledge.
Yet they are bright shining
Multitudinous stars, inlaid
On the skies of the heart.

IV

The orphan boat of my heart
Crosses the unsteady, undulant,
Ocean of Time.

V

The commonplace puddle
Reflects the setting sun
And becomes the Sea of Gold.

VI

Oh little island,
How can you be so secure,
When countless great mountains
Have sunk in the sea?

VII

The rose of Heaven—
Its red appears
In contemplative vision.
The pine branch of Heaven—
Its green appears
In contemplative vision.
But the Word of Heaven
Is neither written nor read
In contemplative vision.

VIII

Bright moon—
All grief, sorrow, loneliness completed—
Fields of silver light—
Who, on the other side of the brook
Blows a surging flute?

IX

A trellis of sticks
Crowned with chrysanthemums—
Right there,
You can realize all
The self-sufficient universe.

PING HSIN

Pai Wei

(1902-)

白薇

MADRID

Madrid—
Blood drops, drip, drop, from the child in your arms.
And Spain is kept awake all night
By this novel apparition
That frightens the old time militants.
You are the splendid future,
The ruthless clean sweep,
That pulls the puppet,
Dragging his black shadow,
Marching towards you from Morocco.

You are a woman in childbirth,
Threatened with puerperal disasters,
Who struggles to protect your newborn baby.
I am afraid that your labor
Will have bled you past saving—
Your labor which has exceeded that of St. Mary.

Cheng Min

(1924?–)

EVENING RENDEZVOUS

I cannot raise my hand
To knock at your door
For fear the sound will not be gentle enough.
A little boat returns
Without the sound of oars
But waits on the tide and the evening sea wind.
If you, sitting under your lamp,
Hear soft breathing outside your door,
And sense someone quietly near you,
Throw away your cigarette
And soundlessly push open the door
You will see me there,
Waiting by your door.

STUDENT

I go one step forward,
Then stumble one step back.
I join the march
And then slip away to the sidelines.
I look at the posters on the left wall,
And the people gathered around them.
I look at the posters on the right wall,
And the people gathered around them.
They are like soldiers in two bunkers,
Shooting at one another
With arrows that fly away over my head.
O Socrates of the streets,
Where are you?
I heard that you can bring the young to face the truth
Like a shepherd who herds his sheep
Onto the right path,
Like a kind passerby
Who returns a lost child to its mother.
But why have you forgotten
This country more baffled than any other country,
This time more doubtful
Than any other time?
Here yes and no are indistinguishable
Like East and West at the Poles.
Here truth is a puppet
That doubles in two roles.
One self says, "Whatever is mine must be truth."
The other says, "When your 'whatever'
Becomes my 'whatever,' then it is truth."
Truth becomes a tasty bait

To lure fish obsessed with books.
In their short sighted, round eyes
They cannot see the many hooks of fraud.
Socrates, if you cannot reappear
In the network of streets
Of the Twentieth Century,
Why cannot Truth become simply a baby
That laughs when it is happy,
And cries when it is hurt,
As if to tell me which is itself?

CHENG MIN

Jung Tzu

(1928–)

紫
蓉
子

MY DRESSING MIRROR IS A HUMPBACKED CAT

My dressing mirror is a humpbacked cat.
Continuously my image changes
As though on flowing water.
A humpbacked cat. A speechless cat.
A lonely cat. My dressing mirror.
A staring, round, startled eye.
A never waking dream wavers inside it.
Time? Radiance? Sorrow?
My dressing mirror is a cat of Fate.
Like a controlling face that locks up
My rich beauty in its own monotony,
My quiet virtue in its coarseness.
Steps, gestures, indolent as a long summer,
Desert its melodic steps,
Immured here in my dressing mirror—
A squatting cat.
A cat. A confused dream.
No light. No shadow.
Never once the reflection
Of my true image.

Lin Ling

(1935–)

林泠

SINKING

Endlessly sinking—
My wings into the waves of your eyes.
How much I hope,
How much I hope,
That we will sink beautifully down,
Into a kingdom forgotten by Apollo,
Where we will walk and leave no footprints,
Just as the rivers there do not rise in the high
   mountains
But originate in the ocean.
That breeze is no more a breeze.
The wood on the hill is no more
A wood on the hill.
We are no more ourselves.
We are dust.
We are everything.
Yet everything again, all in one brief glance
Will be denied all value.
Oh, how I hope. . . .

CLOUD DISSECTS ITSELF

I was born in the old home of the sun,
My tomb will be the blue green ocean,
Just like the tiny meteorite in the sky.
The lights of the fishing boats,
Returning late in the night,
Will be the tears of my mourners.
I always remember,
Many years ago there was a girl
Who loved to dress in red.
She slowly walked through the human world,
With gestures of mist,
With the rhythm of rain,
With the melody of a flowing stream.
And the flames and snowflakes
She scattered so freely
Became the Equator and the North and South Poles.
I always remember—
Like the tiny meteorite in the sky,
The ocean is my emerald tomb,
The lights of the fishing boats,
Homeward bound in the late night,
Are the tear drops of my mourners.

LIN LING

FOOTPATHS CROSS IN
THE RICE FIELD

You are horizontal.
I am vertical.
We divide the heavenly bodies
And the four directions between us.
We come from the place of becoming,
Pass by here,
And encounter each other
In this final meeting
In a flooded rice field.
An egret descends on still wings.
We quietly chat about the weather,
And say, "I'll see you again."
Quietly make an appointment,
Climb two far apart hillsides,
And look back from the summits.
A pure white feather floats down.
As the feather floats down,
Oh, at that moment
We both hope that happiness
May also be like a white bird,
Quietly descending
We hope—
Even though birds
Are creatures with wings.

LIN LING

VAGUE APPREHENSION
to a gambler

On your breast,
In your arms—
O night of Monte Carlo—
The man I love
Warms himself at the fire.
He did not gather enough
Pine branches to make a blaze.
Night of Monte Carlo.
He asks for my hair,
My vertebrae.

LIN LING

WOMAN WALL

I have been expecting it so much.
Only I
Walked in its shadow.

This time, the second time I have come,
I dream no more the vastness.
With hands behind my back,
I walk from one end to the other.
I am thinking—
How can so slight a thread tie up a city?

LIN LING

Tuo Ssu

(1939–)

TRAIN

Completely worn out,
We sleep soundly
As a fisherman's net
Cast into the stillness of noon,
And then we sleep tightly
Rolled up in Time.
One dream left over
From the melody of a broken marriage.
We search for ourselves
Amongst the shadows
On the window panes of a street.
Yesterday's slaves,
Yesterday slaves with unfettered feet.
On the eve of the destruction of the world,
We piously repent.
If we were abandoned in a warm breeze,
If we were exiled from a Kingdom,
Small as a railway platform,
We would lift up our hearts,
Chilly with self pity,
Our eyes holding the limitless concerns of love.
But we are forced to leave the dust of winter
With a more subtle pain.
But in a small boxlike cart
We saw Time coil, unroll, and coil again.
We slept and the wheels
Went on repeating, monotonously
Talking in their sleep,
And the train went on
At the full speed of love,
Lightly caressing the great earth.

SPROUT

You are a mildewed painting.
You are a land that can no longer bear—
With your eccentric face
And your strange temper
Incapable of smiling—
In love with the past—
A dream of yesterday.
A tiny side road
That disrupts a long avenue,
With a red light constantly
Shining its evil eye.
Yesterday's dream is a drawer
Littered with little mice turds.
The quarrelsome clouds of small rain
Are all calm now,
Calm as your breast with
The polished brass buttons
On your old fashioned, classical coat.
And I forget about the weather today,
And the South Wind,
Because you have become a melody;
You live in a black and white keyboard's
Undulating dream of melody.
I am reading poetry.
But I cannot guess
If you can grow in this strange foreign land.
For I hear that new sprouts
Are always tender.

TUO SSU

NIGHT STREET

Withering, shrivelling, dancing,
The wet cold boulevard
Rests after the rain.
A boulevard like a leopard,
Who demands that the night
Give up its melancholy,
Give up its cold silence,
Give up its wind.
A wisp of grass burns in the fire
As dew vanishes in the morning.
You cannot reject the doubt
And perplexity of a virgin.
You can only go straight ahead
Into night's great hall.
Thus, so, the slight smile of the evening clouds
Breaks up into the pebbles of temptation.
A violet of pure love wavers,
And thrusts into the seam.
An automobile presses down the street.
And the street against it falls into night,
Night with lamplight in its mouth—
Lamplight, with its fine mist
Splashing me and teasing me—
The street's mysterious secret
Held in the mouth of night.
Wet cold night—the leopard night,
And all the other forms of night.
Only this higher fullness
Is like a drydock
Which cannot exhale a ship.

TUO SSU

Hsiung Hung

(1940–)

夏
虹

THE PITCHER

You stand over it
Without sadness. It is
A porcelain water pitcher
On the table, just as it was
In the old days,
Just as it was by the rippling spring.
You are without sadness.
You drink the pure sweet water
That it holds.
Deep in the forest
Ten thousand leaves
Shed their lucid brightness.
You pass by there,
And draw the pitcher full of clear water.
Poems come into form there, one by one.
It is always full of the sound of music there,
Of the ceaseless beating of wings.
I am there, one white feather.
Expectation crowds on the table,
As against a shore
Where you cross over
Against the heavy weight of Time
And carry away the pitcher.

SUMMER FREEZES HERE

I am putting you in a painting.
There is a road there like a ribbon,
A long white ribbon stretching
Deep into mist and clouds,
Deep into an embroidered dream,
Twenty miles long,
In a village by the sea.
We can walk there and never tire.
There are icicles where the road
Goes along the edge of the shore.
Summer freezes there.
You are changed into a transparent forest,
Where every single new leaf
Utters a perfumed word.
You know it well,
This land of my white polar heart,
A road twenty miles long that harvests your footsteps.
One white flower.
One white flower.
One white flower.

HSIUNG HUNG

WRITTEN IN THE SUNSET

Time is engraved on the pale green faces
Of the floating lotus leaves.
Our hearts are a sea, a lake,
Finally a little pond, where
Spider webs interlock over the round leaves,
And below them our longing
Is only a single drop of dew.

Sometimes, suddenly the old story overcomes us.
Time triumphs then.
And lets down its hair—
Shadowy black,
Trailing like a willow.

The old melancholy
Comes from the land of longing.
The colors of the sunset thicken.
The shadows grow fast on the water.
You can tear them,
But not tear them away.

HSIUNG HUNG

TO ———

A hand extends toward me
Holding a steel hammer,
Dry, thin, purple like a firefly's light
Hammering my heart strings,
Breaking them.
Then the curtain of mist descends
On the sleeping lotuses.
Deeper and deeper sleeping,
Never waking,
On the cold blue lake,
On that July.

Mist too thin to hide my eyes,
When at midnight
The finger of death touches my lips,
And stops my dying wish,
And I sleep for you forever
Never to awake—
In the lake of oblivion.

                    HSIUNG HUNG

WHO STOPS THE DANCE?

Like wild tea blossoms
One white skirt
Follows another white skirt.
Parasols open like a thousand petals—
Corpses of dreams—
A thousand petals of the falling Spring.
I want to pull you to pieces—
My heart full of weary anxiety.
Who spilled life over this meadow?
Who stopped the dance?
Who smashed the dream?
Who trampled the Spring?
Fate.
Tomorrow you must obey.
Yes, I want to pull you to pieces—
White skirt, white skirt
As weariness and anxiety
Overwhelm my heart.

HSIUNG HUNG

IF YOU THINK WITH FIRE

If you think with fire
Then life is a road that leads
To waiting for nothing.
On its two sides stand wonderful buildings,
Whose compound eyes brim and flow
With happy songs of great mansions,
And the melancholy of little round houses.

Then there sinks to the bottom
Of a trembling white jade cup
The broken necklace of the past,
Two pieces dazzling the eyes
With their red lustre—
July and March.

If the castle where my dreams are stored
Began to burn,
I would stand bewildered in the rain,
Watching one man,
And so wildly,
Thinking of another.

HSIUNG HUNG

THINKING OF SOMEONE

For you I have stored up an ocean of thought,
Quiet, transparent, bright.
Your arms encircle the city of sleep
Of my far off, beautiful dreams.

A lamp shines faintly through a crescent window.
It is your name, changed to gold and silver silk,
That has wrapped me and entangled me
With half a century.

An ocean of thoughts
All stored in that quiet city moat—
The most beautiful language,
Sounds like beautiful flower petals,
That fall and clothe my body with dream.

HSIUNG HUNG

Lan Ling

(1946-)

A MELODY

I

Wind shakes the grass.
Its upright posture
Is torn apart. A voice awakens
The ashes.
The news is written
On vanishing dew.

II

It encircles the reeds and flows
Along the two banks of the stream.
The reflection on the water
Has no light.
Suddenly a splash.
The shadow of a face
Descends like night on stone.

III

Leaning against the wind, he stands.
Grass withers between his brows.
The stars descend into the midnight river,
Emptied by the storm.
He who has never worn shoes
Has gone far away but is still inaudibly near.

THE ARRIVAL

Resting on the alien garden of your forehead,
We, like the morning, dedicate the velvety
Gleam of light that has climbed
Over ten thousand walls,
And fallen into majestic heavenly fire.
Our joyful surprise cannot always be hidden.
Every springtime, after the snow,
Always some old friends
Return unexpectedly,
Bringing the Third Month's melting snow and warmth.
No matter whether you stay a long or short time,
For us your visit begins a time of celebration.
On your forehead we ascend to
The simple purity of your every morning.

LAN LING

BEYOND SILENCE

Tonight let reeds be growing
Along your veins'
Ceaselessly swelling rivers.
The flight of light causes that dark clamour.
Then suddenly all is nothingness,
Only an exposed corpse,
On the naked arm of Time,
In a long alley filled with smoke,
The last heap of evening fire,
Like bells and drums,
Is buried in my self's pale sleep.
A dust storm drives the wind down the road,
And finally arrives
At the early death of an ear of wheat,
And like a river, rises in quiet fury.

LAN LING

from THE WHITE COLOR
OF NEARNESS

Already yesterday's lips have broken
The origin of song.
The sound ends in the sea.
It cannot leap out of
The immensity of death.
In the dark, dark, winter snow,
On the shore, a crane walks by.
Its outspread wings support the space between heaven
    and earth.
Fire of tragic splendor.
A certain kind of martyrdom.
After all, feathers do not decay,
But return to the earth.
It has been promised
That its ghost will flutter,
Fastened to the wind.
In a moment the sunny terrace
Turns wet and cold.
Even the window cannot bypass
The memory of a single glance
In the bottom of a lake.

LAN LING

Tan Ying

(1943–)

DRINKING THE WIND

She is a black crow being driven out of sight.
Her furious cry cannot awaken the flowers.
So she holds under her wings the cold currents
Wandering

on the edge of waters,
And searching beyond the borders—
There is not a tree, nor a song.
That year,
When Autumn perched on her left shoulder,
Snow and homesickness had already
Fallen on her right shoulder.
She is exiled to this icy horizon,
Searching far ahead and behind,
There is no trace of man.
Only her own wandering footprints on the snow
Stretching away to the deep winding corridor of
her mother's eyes.

That year
According to the legend, her footprints were carried by
the West Wind
to the remote River of Oblivion
And her voice melted away with the deep snow.
Not even one among the sixty-four diagrams of the
I Ching could
burn and show a definite oracle.
For she is a black crow cast away beyond memory.
After pecking and breaking a full glass
Of the wine of reunion,
She flies into the night, and with one draught drinks
All the sighs of a thousand miles.

Chung Ling

(1945-)

DUSK ON THE VERANDA BY
LAKE MENDOTA
Summer 1968

Women's or men's hair waltzed with the wind like
    streamers
Hundreds of brimful eyes on the veranda absorbed
    each other

Turning suddenly
I saw you there
Lifting your head from the cards
Smiling readily to me
With the same anticipation
And naked desire

On the border of spring and summer
—from leaf to leaf or ripple to ripple—
The wind smuggled the golds of setting sun
Your lips and nightward pupils
Sparkled

Clapping aimless hands out of my sight
The cloud-dyed lake tended to utter a lost crimson
    song

THE FALL OF MOON LADY
Before the landing of Apollo X

Girl in the moon, are you sorry
You stole the herb of immortality,
And night after night have to
Watch over the distant, emerald
Sea and the boundless jeweled sky?
—Li Shang-yin (813–858)

O stop, Jade Rabbit!
Stop chattering about the cloud-dwelling hills,
The dew-dyed reeds, Li Po's poetry and so on,
Stop dusting with your whiskers the dirt on my
  sleeves.
The dirt was spread from that globe,
It has confiscated my house,
And polluted the mirror of my mind.
I am homeless.

It's the tragedy of us gods
Capable of foreseeing the future.
Tomorrow, shining with metallic pride,
They will arrive to take over my home.
Tomorrow, I will hear from the trial of 4000 years:
Life detention is my sentence.

Don't you see thousands of dead souls
Whirled in black fumes
Hastily coming to mourn over my fate?
As hastily as those long-ceased stars
That bent forward with their gleaming eyes
To stare at my ascension.

Tomorrow I will sink into darkness
Like a wing-broken china bird
Eternally
Falling toward midnight.

CHUNG LING

ON THE MELTING LAKE

I dreamt of walking on icy waves.
I dreamt of the shut-in blue.
Shall we go?

A tin can with an icy tongue inside,
A tin can rolled on the crackling white:
Here I threw out a broken cadence.

The shimmering sun mingled
Its heat with the snow.
You told me,
"It is not a long blue snake,
But the sign of a melting lake.
Soon we will hear its cracking."

CHUNG LING

SONG OF ROOTLESS PEOPLE

Root hanging in the air,
I want to hold you
A handful in my hands.

Last night—riding on
The white sprays of four thousand years—
You came to scratch my snow-flaked window
And strained my morning dream
With a shower of crystal flowers.

O drifting root,
I want to measure the bitterness
Of your every rootlet
I want to dust with my fingers
The dirt hidden in your wrinkles.

But always, just like the snow,
You merely stoop slightly
From eight directions
To touch me with your whisker
And pass me by.

CHUNG LING

VISITING

I make fast my white barge
To the bank of the brimming stream.
The water is silver plated with moonlight.
The green lock on his stone gate
Is picked and smashed.
Ripples are frozen in his eyes.
Dew has faded his ruby lips.
We count the gleams of the fishing boats.
Scattered amongst the foggy ice floes.

Phantom after phantom sits on the ancient barrows
Playing psalteries.
A thousand night blooming cereus
Flake down in the melody.
The rambling clouds stoop clumsily to listen.
When a single string snaps
All the fingers vanish—
Nothing is left but glistening snow petals.

CHUNG LING

Jên Jui

(?–1949)

MIDNIGHT

Midnight. The flowing water of Hu T'o River
Sounds more distinctly.
Suddenly a strong wind blows.
The wind's sound and the water's sound
Together become an enormous roar.
I cannot sleep in peace.
The voices of nature speak
To the troubled hearts of men.
I lie quietly, stilling my heart.
I refuse to remember
The tragic death of the father of my sons.
I refuse to remember
The husband and wife
Embracing, leaning against each other,
Or the sons and daughters around their knees.
I will not imagine
My youngest son's fate on the battlefield.
With all my heart I long for the dawn.
The cruelty of Fascism
The violence and corruption of the enemy
Have turned white the hair of mothers
And wrinkled their foreheads.
At last the dawn comes.
But with it come again
Savage battles, young men falling,
Others taking their places
In heroic sacrifice.
How many of my friends
Are already mothers of martyrs?
Perhaps I am one of them.

Li Chü

(Mid 20th Century)

HARVESTING WHEAT FOR THE PUBLIC SHARE

It is a year of good harvest
The wheat is brought to the threshing yard.
The second sister crushes it.
The elder sister threshes it.
The third sister winnows it
Very carefully and throws away the husks.
The golden grain piles high in the yard.
Round, round wheat, better than pomegranate seeds.
Bite it with your teeth, it goes "go-pou!"
The first pile of wheat is really lovely.
After we have dried it in the sun,
And cleaned it,
We will turn it in as the public share.

I.
Notes to the Poems

ANONYMOUS (fifth century). These are four of twenty-five anonymous poems gathered under the title *Hua Shan Chi.* "On the Slope of Hua Mountain". The curious legends is that a young man was travelling past the slope of Hua Mountain when he saw a beautiful girl and fell in love with her. When he got home he grew sick with unfulfilled love and took to his bed. In desperation his mother went to see the girl who gave her the apron she wore to bring back to the boy. When he saw the apron he swallowed it and died. With his last words he told his mother to leave his coffin in front of the girl's house. When she saw the coffin, the girl spontaneously sang these twenty-five songs, the coffin opened and she lay down beside the youth and died. This legend begins a long tradition in poetry, drama and fiction of ill-fated lovers, most notably Liang Shan-po and Chu Ying-t'ai, though in fact the songs are probably folk song laments. *Hua Shan Chi* became a cliché for a cemetery. *Ch'üan Sung Shih, chüan* 5.

ANONYMOUS (thirteenth-fourteenth centuries). These two poems are examples of the many anonymous popular songs in the Yüan Dynasty sung in the pleasure cities, composed by courtesans or their visitors. *Ch'üan Yüan San Ch'ü,* vol. II, p. 1696.

ANONYMOUS COURTESAN (sixteenth century). *Chung Kuo Fu Nü Wên Hsüeh Shih,* part III, b, chapter 9, p. 57.

CHANG WÊN-CHI (ninth century?), the wife of an official, Pao, was famous for her short quatrains. This could be a political poem. *Ch'üan T'ang Shih, chüan* 799.

CHAO LUAN-LUAN (eighth century?) was an elegant prostitute in the pleasure city of Ch'ang An, the T'ang capital. Her poems were a common type, a sort of advertising copy in praise of the parts of a woman's body, written for courtesans and prostitutes. *Ling hua* are flowers carried by Taoist

Immortals *(hsien)*. In art they are often represented as peonies. *T'an* in the T'ang Dynasty was actually dyewood from Indochina. *Ch'üan T'ang Shih, chüan* 802.

CHENG MIN (b. 1924). During World War II, she was enrolled at the National Southwest University in Kunming, where she studied philosophy. In the early 1950's she studied English literature at Brown University (Providence, R.I.), and returned to the People's Republic of China in 1959. *Shih Chi,* pp. 1, 130.

CHU SHU-CHÊN (early twelfth century). Although she has often been ranked as second only to Li Ch'ing-chao, almost nothing is known with certainty of her life, and all the details of her traditional biography, which seems to have been developed largely from her poems, have been questioned. Her poems were published in 1182 by Wei Chung-kung, who claimed to have collected her poems from copies she had given to her friends (since after her death her parents had burned her own copies). Her father is supposed to have been an official in Chekiang; her husband, whose name is unknown, is thought to have been either a merchant or a minor official, and the poet Lady Wei is said to have been her friend; but even her approximate date has been disputed. There are other poems by her in Rexroth's *100 Poems from the Chinese. Ch'üan Sung Tz'ŭ,* vol. II, pp. 1405–1408; *Chu Shu Chên Tuan Ch'ang Shih Tz'ŭ.*

CHU CHUNG-HSIEN (fifteenth century), also known as Chu Miao-tuan, was a native of Chekiang Province, the daughter of the court official Chu Tsu, and the wife of a county school official of low rank. *Ming Yüan Shih Hsüan Ts'ui Lou Chi,* pp. 23–24; *Chung Kuo Fu Nü Wên Hsüeh Shih Hua,* part III, b, chapter 3, p. 16.

CHUNG LING (b. 1945), the cotranslator of this anthology, was born in Chungking and grew up in Taiwan. She came to the United States in 1967, where she completed a Ph.D. in Comparative Literature at the University of Wisconsin, Madison. She now works at the State University of New York, Albany.

THE FALL OF MOON LADY. According to legend, the great archer Ih shot down nine suns from the sky to save the people from devastating drought. Around 2190 B.C. he became ruler of China; he obtained the elixir of immortality from the Queen Goddess of the West, but his beautiful wife, Ch'ang-O, stole it and flew to the moon. *Hsing Tso*, No. 13, p. 69; *Ch'un Wên Hsüeh*, No. 35, p. 98; *Hsien Tai Wên Hsüeh*, No. 35, pp. 120–121; *Yu Shih Wên I*, No. 209, p. 57; *Ming Pao Monthly*, vol. IV, No. 10, p. 19.

CHUO WÊN-CHÜN (179?–117? B.C.) is one of the most famous lovers in Chinese history. The daughter of a wealthy man in Szechuan, she was widowed at seventeen, whereupon Ssu-ma Hsiang-ju, a poor writer, fell in love with her. He played the psaltery and sang to her at a banquet given by her father and she eloped with him. Disowned and poverty-stricken, they opened a wine shop. This so humiliated her father that he gave them a large sum of money. Ssu-ma Hsiang-ju became famous, the leading court poet of the Emperor Wu of Han and took a concubine. Broken-hearted, Chuo Wên-chün wrote A SONG OF WHITE HAIR which so moved her husband that he gave up the concubine and returned to her. This story is probably pure legend. In many collections the poem is anonymous. *Ch'üan Han Shih, chüan* 4; or, *Ku Shih Yüan, chüan* 2; or, *Ku Shih Hsüan, chüan* 1.

CH'IEN TAO (early eleventh century) was a concubine of K'ou Chun (961–1023), a prime minister of Sung. Two of her poems survive. The other is translated in Rexroth's *Love and the Turning Year. Ku Chin T'u Shu Chi Ch'êng*, vol. 420, *kui yüan tien, chüan* 335, *kui tsao pu; Chung Kuo Fu Nü Wên Hsüeh Shih Hua*, part III, a, chapter 5, p. 31.

CH'IU CHIN (1879?–1907) was the daughter of a lawyer and a secretary in the local government. At eighteen she married Wang T'ing-chün. After the birth of her children she left her family in 1904 and went to Japan to study; there she joined Sun Yat-sen's revolutionary party and soon rose to the leadership. In 1906 she returned to teach school and founded a newspaper for women in Shanghai. In the next year she joined the staff of the school, which served as the secret headquarters and arsenal for the revolutionary army. In June of that year she was arrested by the Manchu government. In her trial her poems were used as evidence of treason and she was beheaded on July 15, 1907, less than five years before the overthrow of the Manchu Dynasty. Kiang Kang-hu, translator with Witter Bynner of *The Jade Mountain* (The 300 Poems of T'ang), was her friend. Her poetry, like that of Chairman Mao and many other revolutionaries after her, is classical in style and shows little Western influence.

To the tune "The River is Red." Ch'in Liang-yü was a seventeenth-century heroine who, after the death of her husband, was appointed commander of his army. Shen Yün-yin (seventeenth century), after her father was killed by the rebel army of Chang Hsiang-chung, took command, defeated them and recaptured her father's body.

A LETTER TO LADY T'AO CH'IU YIN HAO (fourth century) was unfairly banished from the court. Back home in his study he wrote ideograms in the air expressing his frustration. *Ch'iu Chin Chi,* pp. 77, 110, 111.

HAN TS'UI-PIN (ninth century). This poem is attributed to Han, a palace woman of the Emperor Hsüan of T'ang (847–873). As the scholar Lu walked by the palace moat, he picked up a red leaf floating on the water with this poem written on it. Later, when the palace released some women, Lu married the one who saw the leaf and recognized it as the poem she had written. There are four poems with a similar story of a red leaf in the *Ch'üan T'ang Shih* (The Complete Collection of T'ang Poetry). *Ch'üan T'ang Shih, chüan* 797.

LADY HO (300 B.C.) was the wife of Han P'in, a retainer of Duke Yüan of Sung (reign 326–288 B.C.) who arrested Han and forced Lady Ho to marry him. She wrote this SONG OF MAGPIES and hung herself. *Ku Shih Yüan, chüan* 1.

HO SHUANG-CH'ING (1712–?) was a native of Chiangsu Province, and came from a family of farmers. She learned to read and write from her uncle, a teacher in a country school. She exchanged her embroidery for books of poetry. At eighteen she married a farmer of the Chou family in a nearby town. Her husband was illiterate, had a bad temper and treated her cruelly, and her mother-in-law often tortured her. *Chung Hua Li Tai Fu Nü*, pp. 312–313; *Chung Kuo Fu Nü Wên Hsüeh Shih Hua*, p. 98.

HSIUNG HUNG (b. 1940) is the pen name of Hu Mei-tzu, born in Taiwan. She received a degree in fine arts from National Taiwan Normal University, and now works as a designer in Taiwan. *Chin Yung*, pp. 4, 22, 32, 68, 74, 92, 112.

HSÜEH CH'IUNG (eighth or ninth century). Nothing is known about her, other than that she lived under the T'ang Dynasty. The Ch'u Kingdom that fell in 233 B.C. was in today's Hupei Province. *Ch'üan T'ang Shih, chüan* 801.

HSÜEH T'AO (768–831) was the best known woman poet of the T'ang Dynasty. In her childhood she moved from Ch'ang An to Szechuan where her father had a government appointment. She became well known as a poet at an early age, and was honored at the banquets and poetry contests given by the governor of Szechuan. She was a friend of the leading poets of her day, Po Chü-i, Yüan Chên and Liu Yü-hsi, who all admired her. Later in life she moved to Washing Flower Creek where she produced fine paper for poetry. Amy Lowell used the name of this paper, "fir flower tablets," as the title of the book of Chinese translations she did with Florence Ayscough.

AN OLD POEM TO YÜAN CHÊN. In the T'ang Dynasty it was a custom for the winning candidate in the imperial examinations to go to the pleasure city in the capital and celebrate his success by writing poems on fine red paper to the leading courtesans. *Ch'üan T'ang Shih, chüan* 803.

LADY HUA JUI (tenth century) was the wife of Mêng Hsu, the king of Szechuan, who adored her and called her Lady of the *hua jui* ("flower pistil"). In 965 he was defeated by the army of Emperor T'ai, the first emperor of Sung, and died soon after his surrender. Lady Hua Jui was taken by the emperor for his harem. *Ch'üan T'ang Shih, chüan* 798.

HUANG O (1498–1569) was the daughter of Huang Ko, President of the Board of Works in the Ming Court. In 1519 she married Yang Shen, a poet and dramatist. Their marriage was said to be a very happy one. The attitude of the Chinese government toward erotic literature was unusually permissive during the early sixteenth century, the time of great erotic novels like the *Chin P'ing Mei* and extremely bawdy comedies in the theater. Even so, overtly erotic poetry was not considered the province of women writers who were not courtesans. Huang O was unique.

To the tune "Soaring Clouds." Rhinoceros horn is supposed to be the most powerful aphrodisiac (although in fact it is inert). *Huang Fu Jen Yüeh Fu; Chung Kuo Nü Hsin Ti Wên Hsüeh Shêng Huo,* pp. 328–334.

JÊN JUI (d. 1949), a revolutionary since the turn of the century, participated when still a young girl in the overthrow of the Manchu Dynasty and between 1910 and 1920 joined the May Fourth Movement and later the Communist Party. Her husband, also a Party member, was killed by the Kuomintang. She had five children. In 1949, the year the People's Republic was established, she died of stomach disease.

MIDNIGHT was written in August, 1949, on the shore of the Hu T'o River which flows from Shanhsi Province to Hopei Province and debouches into the ocean passing by T'ientsin. *Chung Kuo Fu Nü,* No. 18, 1959, p. 21.

JUNG TZU (b. 1928) was born in Chiangsu, is married to the poet Lo Men, and lives in Taiwan. She has published several books of verse and has won poetry prizes. A book of poems of Jung Tzu ("hibiscus") and Lo Men has been translated into English. *Ch'i Shih Nien Tai Shih Hsüan,* p. 246.

KUAN P'AN-P'AN (eighth or ninth century) was a great courtesan in Hsü Chou. The statesman Chang Chien took her as his concubine and built for her the Swallow Mansion, a sumptuous palace. They ran a salon where they entertained notables, including such leading poets of the time as Po Chü-i. After Chang died, P'an-p'an lived on, and Po wrote poems asking why she did not die with her lord. The poem translated is one of three in answer to him. She told Po that she did not die with Chang because she felt her death might blemish his reputation. After fifteen years had elapsed she decided that it was time to die and committed suicide in Swallow Mansion. She is mentioned later as a heroine by many poets including Su Tung-p'o and Ch'in Kuan. The words *chien lü* are omitted in the translation. They mean "sword, shoes" and allude to courtiers so favored by the emperor that they did not have to remove their swords and shoes in the audience chamber. *Ch'üan T'ang Shih, chüan* 802.

KUAN TAO-SHÊNG (1262–1319) was the wife of one of the leading calligraphers and painters of Chinese history, Chao Mêng-fu, and herself famed as a calligrapher and painter of bamboos, orchids, and plum blossoms. Liu Ta-pei's *Chiu Shih Hsin Hua.*

LAN LING (b. 1946) was born in the Philippines and has an M.F.A. from the Creative Writing Workshop at the University of Iowa. She lives with her husband, a physician of Chinese descent from the Philippines, in Iowa City. *Unpublished manuscript.*

LI CHÜ (mid-twentieth century) is a member of the farm commune of Ta Yeh District in the Teng-fung county of Honan Province. *Chung Kuo Fu Nü,* No. 9, 1958, p. 13.

LI CH'ING-CHAO (1084–1151) is universally considered to be China's greatest woman poet. She and her husband Chao Ming-ch'eng came from well-known families of scholars and officials. Li's mother had some reputation as a poet, and her father was a friend of Su Tung-p'o. Li and Chao were an ideal literary couple. They had poetry contests with each other and with their literary friends. They were not only poets but scholars and collectors and spent most of their money to build up a vast collection of seals, bronzes, manuscripts, calligraphy and paintings, and compiled the best critical study and anthology of seals and bronze characters ever written. When in 1127 the army of Chin Tatars invaded Sung China, they were driven from their home in Ch'ing Chou (in today's Shantung Province) and lost most of their collection—the contents of ten buildings were burned. In 1129 when Li was forty-six, her husband went alone to a new official post in today's Chekiang and was taken ill on the way. Li hastened to him, but he died in an inn shortly after she reached him. After her husband's death she lived alone, usually in flight, striving to save what was left of their collection while the Chin were driving the Sung out of North China. Seven of her poems are translated in Rexroth's *100 Poems from the Chinese;* six others appear in *Love and the Turning Year.* Her work is not to be confused with the formularized, deserted-courtesan and abandoned-wife poems so common in Chinese poetry, and usually written by men—for instance, Li Po's "Jewelled Stairs Grievance" (translated by Ezra Pound). Her poems are truly personal utterances, comparable to those of Gaspara Stampa and Louise Labé in the West. They fall into three groups: the period of happily married life; that of desolation at the death of her husband; and that of increasing loneliness as she grew old.

THE SORROW OF DEPARTURE. There is another version of the first five lines of this poem. This translation is based on the one in *Hua An Tz'ŭ Hsüan.*

To the tune "A Hilly Garden." Lord of Spring is *tung chün,* "East God," the god of Spring used as a metaphor of the man she loves.

SPRING ENDS. *Shuang hsi* ("two rivers") is in today's Chekiang Province; in her old age Li Ch'ing-chao lived for a while in the nearby town of Chin Hua.

To the tune "The Honor of a Fisherman." There is no other poem like this written by a woman in Chinese literature. It is a poem of mystical trance directly descended from the *Li Sao* (Encountering Sorrow) of Ch'ü Yüan of the fourth century B.C., the shamanist poems, *Ch'u Tz'u* (*Songs of the South,* translated by David Hawkes), and the mystical, Taoist, alchemical writings of Ko-hung of the Three Kingdoms. Illustrations taken originally from a treatise of Ko-hung can be found, misinterpreted, in Carl Jung's *Secret of the Golden*

Flower, and in Leo Wieger's *History of the Religious Beliefs and Philosophical Opinions of China,* Fifty-second Lesson. Sung Dynasty Taoist adepts often induced cosmic visions of this kind by eating the sacred mushroom.

"The huge roc bird," a favorite Taoist legendary creature, can be equated with what we now know to be the autonomic nervous system; the little boat with the Serpent Power, hidden in the perineal plexus, and the Immortal Islands in the East with the thousand-petaled lotus of Indian Yoga. (The three mountains in the Eastern Sea are the paradisal home of the Taoist Immortals.) During the brief period of stability of the Kuomintang regime in Nanking, poems like this and the *Songs of the South* interpreted in terms of erotic mysticism were very fashionable in the more sophisticated intellectual circles, especially in Shanghai. The secret key was considered to be the sixth chapter of the *Tao Te Ching (The Way and Its Power).* This poem raises the question: How many of Li Ching-chao's "love poems" are, like those of Hafiz or Dante, actually mystical?

To the tune "Eternal Happiness." The capital of Northern Sung was in Pien in Chung Chao. Defeated by the Chin, the Sung moved the capital south to present-day Nanking. Presumably Li wrote this poem in Nanking, recalling days in the lost capital. The Feast of Lights occurred on the fifteenth of the First Month, when people competed with beautiful lanterns and showed off their clothing and ornaments, gifts of the New Year.

To the tune "I Paint My Lips Red." Since this poem is about a prostitute receiving one guest after another it is most unlikely to be by Li Ch'ing-chao, although it is sometimes attributed to her. "Kicking the swing" is an obvious cliché for sexual intercourse.

To the tune "Picking Mulberries." Attributed to Li Ch'ing-chao. *Ling hua ching* is either an octagonal bronze mirror or one ornamented with water flowers on the back. On the best highly polished bronze mirrors of the T'ang period, the ornament shows through like a faint ghost on the mirror surface. *Ch'üan Sung Tz'ŭ,* vol. II, pp. 925–934; *Li Ch'ing-chao Chi.*

LI YEH (eighth century) was a Taoist priestess renowned for her beauty, wit, poetry, calligraphy, and her skill on the psaltery. The poets Liu Chang-ch'ing, Chiao Jan and Lu Yü were her close friends. When she was an old lady she was summoned to the court by the emperor Hsüan of T'ang. T'ao Ch'ien (373–427), one of China's major poets, wrote much in praise of nature and of wine. Hsieh Ling-yün (385–433) (*hsieh k'ê*, "the Grateful Guest," was his nickname) wrote poems in praise of nature and of wandering among the hills. *Ch'üan T'ang Shih, chüan* 805.

LIN LING (b. 1935) means "cool woods." The poet's real name is Hu Yün-shang. She started to write poetry and essays around 1950. In 1958 she came to the United States to study and has published little since. *Shih Ch'uang Tso Chi,* pp. 77–81; *Liu Shih Nien Tai Shih Hsüan,* pp. 39–42.

MA HSIANG-LAN (sixteenth century), also known as Ma Shou-chen, was the leading courtesan of her time in Chin Ling (Nanking). She was a painter of orchids as well as a poet. *Chung Hsiang Tz'ü,* a photocopy of 1690 edition, 1933; *Chung Hua Li Tai Fu Nü,* p. 430.

MÊNG CHU (third century). Ten verses are attributed to Mêng Chu, but they are probably ancient folk songs from what are today the provinces of Hunan and Hupei. *Ch'üan Chin Shih, chüan* 8.

NIEH SHÊNG-CH'IUNG (Sung Dynasty) was a courtesan in the pleasure city of Ch'ang An, the ancient capital, who later married Li Chih-wen.

To the tune "Partridge Sky." "Phoenix City" is a set phrase for the capital. *Lien hua lou* (Lotus Flower Terrace) is a typical name for a "mansion for courtesans"—a very expensive brothel. *Yang Kuang Chü,* "Song of Sun Pass," was a well-known song of farewell from the T'ang Dynasty. There are several places named Yang Kuang; the one meant is south of Tun Huang in Kansu, the gateway to Central Asia. *Ch'üan Sung Tz'ü,* vol. II, p. 1046.

PAI WEI (b. 1902), "white fern"; her real name is Huang Su-ju. She was born in Hunan and as a young girl ran away to avoid an arranged marriage. In the 1920's she went to Japan to study and was the lover of the poet Yang Sao. Later she became a Communist and now lives in the People's Republic. Between the wars she wrote several popular novels and a verse drama. *Chung Kuo Hsin Wên Hsüeh Ta Hsi Hsü Pien,* vol. 8, p. 427.

PAN CHIEH-YÜ (first century B.C.) is a title of honor given to an imperial concubine. Her given name is unknown. She was the daughter of an official, chosen for the palace of the Emperor Ch'eng of Han (reigned 32– B.C.). For a while she was his favorite, but then he favored Chao Fei-yen. Famous for her delicate beauty and her cunning, Chao Fei-yen plotted against the empress and Pan; the empress was executed but Pan was spared and was permitted to become an attendent of the emperor's mother. After his death she became an attendent in the Imperial Tombs. The "doubled fan of union and joy" is translated from *hê huan shan,* a round fan of two layers glued together. *Hê huan* has a sexual connotation. *Ku Shih Yüan, chüan* 2; *Ku Shih Hsüan, chüan* 1; *Ch'üan Han Shih, chüan* 3.

PAO LING-HUI (fifth century) was the younger sister of the poet Pao Chao (414–466). Her poem imitates one of the anonymous *19 Han Poems* which Ezra Pound translated in *Cathay* and titled "The Beautiful Toilet," and which he mistakenly attributed to Mei Sheng. *Ch'üan Sung Shih, chüan* 5.

PING HSIN (b. 1900) was born in Fukien, the daughter of a naval officer. Her real name is Hsieh Wang-ying; the pseudonym Ping Hsin means "Ice Heart." She was educated in missionary schools and colleges in Peking but before that had read widely in the classical literature in her family's library. After she was graduated from Yenching University in 1923 she took an M.A. from Wellesley, then returned to China and taught at Yenching. In 1929 she married the Chinese sociologist Wu Wen-tsao. In 1951 they returned to the People's

Republic from Japan, where he had been an advisor on the staff of the Mission of the Taiwan government. Up to the Cultural Revolution in 1964 she was an active member of many Chinese Communist literary organizations, but after the 1920's wrote little poetry.

MULTITUDINOUS STARS AND SPRING WATERS, II. The veil of stars is the net or web of Indra, Vairocana, P'a-lu-che-ma, or Dainichi in which all things (and all Buddha worlds) reflect one another infinitely. Also see *Tao Te Ching,* chapter seventy-two: "The net of heaven is all-embracing." VII. *Meng hun,* "dream soul," vision, trance. "Rose," "pine branch," "word of Heaven"—the archetypes. VIII. *Yu yu yang yang,* "up and down soft and loud." *Ping Hsin Shih Chi,* pp. 31–32; 45–46; *"fan hsin"* Nos. 19, 49, 117, 185. *"Ch'un shui"* Nos. 23, 24, 25, 37, 179.

SHAO FEI-FEI (seventeenth century) grew up in Hsi Hu (West Lake), noted for its beautiful scenery and beautiful women. Her father died when she was a child; she and her mother were supported by her uncle. She grew up to be beautiful and talented. An official, Lo, paid a great sum to her mother to take Fei-fei as his concubine and took her home to the North. According to her other poems, it would seem she was remarried, possibly by Lo's jealous wife, to a groom. *Chung Hua Li Tai Fu Nü,* p. 310; *Chung Kuo Fu Nü Shêng Huo Shih,* p. 291.

SU HSAIO-HSAIO (late fifth century) is a legendary courtesan of Hang Chou in Chekiang, reputed to have been one of the two most beautiful women who ever lived. (The other was Yang Kuei-fei, who probably by current standards would be considered obese.) Her tomb shrine still stands by West Lake, itself reputedly the most beautiful spot in China. Hsi-ling Lake is across the Ch'ien T'ang River from Hang Chou near the ancient town of the same name. In the Sung Dynasty there was another Su Hsaio-hsaio, a courtesan in Hang Chou, in legend and in the Chinese popular theater (where the two women were confused) said to have been the mistress of Su Tung-p'o, a circumstance for which there is no accepted evidence. However, the Su Hsaio-hsaio plays are very moving.

At least one movie has been made about her. *Yü T'ai Hsin Yung*, chüan 10; *Ch'üan Ch'i Shih*, chüan 4.

SUN TAO-HSÜAN (early twelfth century) became a widow at thirty and never remarried. In her old age she burned all her poems, but her son, Huang Chu, collected some that had circulated in manuscript. *Ch'üan Sung Tz'ü*, vol. II, p. 1248.

SUN YÜN-FENG (1764–1814) was a native of Chekiang, the daughter of an official, Sung Chia-Lo. She married the scholar Ch'en and was one of the favorites among the thirteen women students of the leading Ch'ing Dynasty poet Yüan Mei. *Ch'ing Tai Fu Nü Wên Hsüeh*, pp. 98–99; *Sui Yüan Nü Ti Tzu Shih.*

TAN YING (b. 1943) is the pen name of Liu Pao-chen, who was born in Malaysia. She was graduated from National Taiwan University, received her M.A. at the University of Wisconsin, and now teaches Chinese at the University of California, Santa Barbara. She has had two collections of poetry published. *Hsing Tso*, No. 13, p. 68.

TUO SSU (b. 1939), "flower thought," is the pen name of Chou Ts'ui-Ch'ing. Her husband Pi Chia is also a poet. She has published novels and a collection of poems, *Profile*, in Taiwan. *Ch'i Shih Nien Tai Shih Hsüan*, pp. 55–57.

TZŬ YEH (third-fourth century). There are forty-two poems in the *Tzŭ Yeh Ko* (The Songs of Tzŭ Yeh) attributed to a girl, Tzŭ Yeh. It is possible there was an original poem and melody composed by her, but the *Tzŭ Yeh* are popular folk songs of Wu, today's Kiangsu and Chekiang provinces. From the fourth to the ninth centuries the style of these poems was widely imitated—by Li Po, among others. *Ch'üan Chin Shih*, chüan 8; *Yüeh Fu Shih Chi*, chüan 44.

T'ANG WAN (twelfth century) was the first wife of the Sung poet Lu Yü (1125–1209). Her mother-in-law disliked her and sent her away, so she married the scholar Chao Shi-chen. One spring day she and Chao gave a party in the Shen Gardens. Lu happened to be in the garden and Chao sent him food and wine. Lu wrote a poem called "Phoenix Hairpin" on the wall of the garden, lamenting his broken marriage; it became one of the most popular *tz'ŭ* poems. Lady T'ang wrote this poem to the same tune in answer. In his old age Lu visited the Shen Gardens again and wrote several poems to his former wife, who by that time had died. *Ch'üan Sung Tz'ŭ*, vol. III, p. 1602.

TS'AI YEN (162?–239?) is traditionally the first great woman poet in Chinese history. She was the daughter of the writer Ts'ai I, the friend of Ts'ao Ts'ao, the warlord of the Three Kingdoms period, and founder through his son of the Wei Dynasty. Around 195 she—then a widow—was captured by the Huns and taken to the North, where she became the concubine of a Hunnish chieftain and bore him two sons. Some years later Ts'ao Ts'ao ransomed her, and married her to one of his officers. Her two sons were left behind. *Hu* is translated as "Tatar," although actually these *Hu* were probably Huns. *Ch'üan Han Shih, chüan* 3.

WANG CH'ING-HUI (end of Sung Dynasty) is reputed to have been the superintendent of ceremonies of the Women's Quarter in the palace of the last emperors of the Sung Dynasty when in 1276 Kublai Khan's army took Hang Chou, the capital of Southern Sung. She was carried away to the north with the emperor and the palace women by the Mongols and is supposed to have written this poem on the wall of a post house. However, it is also attributed to another palace woman, Chang Ch'un-ying. The poem is one of the best of a long tradition of poems by women captured in wars with the peoples of Central Asia of which those by Ts'ai Yen were the first. A popular interpretation of the last line is "I wish the moon (maiden Ch'ang-O) would grant me a fate like hers and that there will be times of deprivation but also times of fullness." *Ch'üan Sung Tz'ŭ*, vol. V, p. 3344.

WANG WEI (seventeenth century) became an orphan when she was seven years old and grew up to be a courtesan and poet in Yang Chou. She married twice and in old age, after her husbands had died, she became a priestess and called herself "Taoist Master in the Straw Coat." She loved to travel with her library on a little boat through the waterways

of Central China, and she is considered one of the best
women poets of nature. She is not to be confused with the
great T'ang Dynasty poet and painter Wang Wei. The *wei's*
are different characters—her, Matthews 7061, "small"; his,
Matthews 7067, "to hold fast." *Chung Kuo Fu Nü Wên Hsüeh
Shih,* part III, b, chapter 9, p. 62.

LADY WEI (late eleventh–early twelfth centuries) was the
wife of the statesman Tseng Pu (1035–1107). The philosopher Chu Hsi (1130–1200) considered her and Li Ch'ing-chao
the best Sung women poets. *Ch'üan Sung Tz'ü,* vol. I, p. 268.

WU TSAO (1800?) was the daughter of a merchant and the
wife of another, both of whom treated her with scant sym-
pathy or understanding and she soon lost interest in males.
She had many female friends and lovers, and wrote erotic
poems to several courtesans. She was very popular in her
lifetime, and her songs were sung all over China. About 1837
she moved to a secluded place and became a Taoist priestess.
Her style is colloquial and fluent, and unlike most Chinese
women poets, she dealt with a wide range of subjects. She is
one of the great Lesbian poets of all time, perhaps not as great
as Sappho, but certainly greater than any modern ones. The
Western woman she most resembles is Lou Andreas Salome.
Wu Tsao is usually regarded as the third woman poet of
China, after Li Ch'ing-chao and Chu Shu-chên, and with
Na-lan Hsin-tê as one of the two leading *tz'ü* poets of the
Ch'ing (Manchu) Dynasty.

IN THE HOME OF THE SCHOLAR WU SU-CHIANG
FROM HSIN AN is written to the tune *"man chiang hung "*
(The River Is Red). Hsieh Fang-tê (thirteenth century)
was a general of the Sung Dynasty who, after his defeat
by the Mongols, lived in disguise as a fortune teller. When
the Mongols had consolidated their rule over all of China
they sought him out and offered him a high official post.
To escape this honor he starved himself to death. The poem
by Tu Fu mentioned in Wu's poem is *"wu chia pieh"* (Alone
without a Home), wherein the man returns to his village
after the long war and discovers it has become a ghost
town.

To the tune "The Pain of Lovesickness." The sound of rain falling on banana leaves is a conventional expression of melancholy, and often of homesickness. It appears in many poems, one of the most notable by Li Ch'ing-chao.

FOR THE COURTESAN CH'ING LIN. The common image of a woman leaning against bamboos living in a valley is an allusion to Tu Fu's poem *"chia jen"* (about a beauty deserted by her husband, living alone in a lonely valley), and occurs elsewhere applied to courtesans longing for their special lovers in the elegant brothel garden. *"Sao mei tsai,"* "paint brow talent" is an epithet for women poets. "Let me buy a red painted boat and carry you away" refers to the fifth-century general Fan Li who, after helping the king of Yüeh defeat the king of Wu, took the beauty Hsi Shih away in a red painted boat; they spent the rest of their lives traveling on lakes and rivers. A very beautiful play has been written on this subject.

To the tune "The Joy of Peace and Brightness." *"Ch'iung lou"* means "splendid tower." The similar expression *"yü lou,"* "jasper or chalcedony tower," means "beautiful shoulders."

To the tune "Flowers Along the Path." The Autumn Feast of the Dead is *Ch'ung Yang,* the Ninth Day of the Ninth Month when it was the popular custom to climb hills or mountains—originally the grave mounds—and have a picnic. In some provinces, as in Canton, the family graves themselves are still visited and decorated with chrysanthemums, a custom which has spread across Europe on All Souls Day. The use of the strings of the psaltery as a metaphor for the years of one's age is an allusion to a cryptic but famous poem by the late T'ang Dynasty poet Li Shang-yin: RETURNING FROM FLOWER LAW MOUNTAIN—"millions of years of decline" —we are entering the Kaliyuga, when the universe runs down. "Flower Law" is the Avatamsaka Sutra *Hsiao T'an Luan Shih Hui Kê Kui Hsiu Tz'ü Hsüeh Hsaiso Ts'ungh Shu.*

EMPRESS WU TSE-TIEN (624–705) was the only empress to rule alone in Chinese history (Tz'u Hsi, the Empress Dowager, the last ruler of the Ch'ing Dynasty, ruled while puppets occupied the throne). She has been compared to Queen Elizabeth I, but she is more like Empress Catherine the Great of Russia. She was first the concubine of the Emperor T'ai of T'ang, and on his death in 649, his son, the Emperor Kao, took her as his concubine. In 655 he dismissed his empress and replaced her with Wu, and from then on she was the actual ruler. In 683 the Emperor died. She permittted no one to take his place on the throne; in 689 she proclaimed herself Empress Wu Tse-t'ien of Chou, and reigned alone from 689–705. After the death of the Emperor Kao she openly kept a male harem, just as the emperors had kept concubines, and also had many lovers among her courtiers. At the same time she was a strong and powerful ruler who knew how to appoint able advisors and ministers. *Ch'üan T'ang Shih, chüan* 5.

Yü Ch'ing-tsêng (nineteenth century) was the grand-daughter of the scholar Yü Yüeh. She married a young, promising poet-scholar, Tsung Sun-nien. People regarded them as an enviable couple: two young, good-looking poets. Unfortunately her mother-in-law was jealous and treated her badly. She is said to have committed suicide.

To the tune "Intoxicated with Shadows of Flowers." The incense clock was a tablet with incense (not the smoke) in the shape of seal characters, usually a two-word "motto," as on Western sundials. The mirror is a long, narrow, horizontal mirror parallel to the bed. *Hsiao T'an Luan Shih Hui K'ê Kui Hsia Tz'ü,* Book 9.

Yü Hsüan-chi (mid-ninth century) was born in Ch'ang An about 860 and became the concubine of an official, Li Yi. His wife was jealous, tortured her and drove her from the house. She became a Taoist priestess, traveled widely, and had many lovers, including the poets Wên Fei-ch'ing and Li Tzu-an. She was accused of murdering her maid, and although her poet friends tried to save her, she was executed about 870.

ADVICE TO A NEIGHBOR GIRL. Sung Yü (third century B.C.) was famed for his good looks and his prose poems, *fu.* "Someone who will never come back" in the original is

Wang Ch'ang, a handsome officer of the T'ang Dynasty. There are poems about the hopeless love of the wife of Lu for Wang.

LIVING IN THE SUMMER MOUNTAINS. Wine cups are floated on streams on Purification Day in the Third Month and people drink wine and write poetry.

ON A VISIT TO CHUNG-CHEN TAOIST TEMPLE. With very few exceptions in the entire history of China, the Imperial Examinations were closed to women. *Ch'üan T'ang Shih, chüan* 804.

II
Chinese Women and Literature
—A Brief Survey

Writing poetry was an essential part of the education and the social life of any educated man in ancient China, but it was not so for a woman. Most of the poems of those who did write were not handed down to posterity. Many women's poems were shown only to their intimates, but were never published. In some cases, the poet herself (Sun Tao-hsüan), or the parents of the poet (Chu Shu-chên), destroyed her work so that the reputation of the clan would not be damaged. Love poems usually led to gossip that the author was an unfaithful wife. Not until the Ch'ing Dynasty (1644-1911) with the promotion of several leading (male) scholars such as Yüan Mei and Ch'en Wên-shu, did writing poetry become fashionable for ladies of the scholar gentry class.

According to the *Li Chi (The Book of Rites)*, supposedly edited by Confucius, a girl of seven was to be separated from males except her closest relatives, and at ten years confined to the women's quarters.[1] The daughters of farmers, artisans, and merchants had more freedom in movement than upper-class women and helped their parents in the fields and shops. The daughters of imperial bureaucrats could travel only in closely curtained sedan-chairs or carts on visits to relatives or temples, and their experience of nature was limited to the gardens of the women's quarters.

Since marriages were pre-arranged, the couple seldom saw each other until their wedding. If the bridegroom did not like the girl, he could later take concubines. But the bride was permanently and exclusively tied to the caprice of her husband. Romantic love occurred rarely, but the occasional evidence of deep marital love, even after years of separation, is remarkable. Usually the woman gave most of her affection to her sons. Sometimes she turned into a fiercely jealous

---

1. *Li Chi*. Taipei, 1965, *chüan* 8, chapter 12, *"nei tse,"* "regulations of the interior."

wife.[2] A couple like Li Ch'ing-chao and Chao Ming-ch'eng, who had mutual respect and understanding for each other's talents and who collaborated in scholarly work, was uncommon. The poetry of Chu Shu-chên, Ho Shuang-ch'ing and Wu Tsao reflects unhappy marriage.

Women were not only intellectually and emotionally isolated, but often physically as well, and might not see their husbands for long periods—often years. A husband might leave his wife behind at home to join the army, to take examinations at the capital, go on business trips, travel with friends to scenic spots, or to take up a post in another province. Songs of farewell and loneliness occupy a great part of women's poetry. The most vivid poet among these forlorn ladies is Chu Shu-chên. Since the second century A.D. numerous male poets, including Li Po and Su Tung-p'o, wrote poems in the persona of a disconsolate woman.

The mother-in-law had almost absolute power over the bride, whose task it was to serve food to her mother-in-law and comb her hair. When a son was newly wed he might spend too much time with his bride, and his mother would become jealous. Lu Yü's wife, Tang Wan, was said to have been driven out of the family by her mother-in-law.

In the Chinese social system only male descendants could perform the ceremony of ancestor worship. Although they bore the heirs, women were secondary in the continuity of the family. A woman belonged to the family of her husband, not to her parents. A daughter had to be provided with food, clothing, a dowry, and a husband found for her. In poor families female infanticide was practiced at least as early as the Han Dynasty (206 B.C.–219 A.D.).[3]

The laws of the T'ang Dynasty reflect the inferior status of wives and concubines:

> If a husband assaults and injures his wife, his punishment
> will be two grades lighter than the normal punishment
> meted for such a crime. . . . If a husband assaults and

---

2. According to another ancient book of rites, *I Li*, Taipei, 1965, in chapter *"sang fu,"* one of the seven reasons to divorce a wife is her jealousy. Many stories tell how famous officials suffered from jealous wives because their wives would not let them take concubines.

3. Ch'en Yung-yuan, *Chung Kuo Fu Nü Shêng Huo Shih* (a history of the lives of Chinese women), Taipei, 1965, p. 61.

badly injures his concubine, his punishment will be two grades lighter than the punishment for injuring his wife.

If a wife assualts her husband she will perform slave labor for one year. [This is punishment seven grades heavier than for the male.] If the husband is seriously injured, her sentence will be three grades heavier than the punishment for heavy assault and injury [which means she will perform slave labor for two years, a punishment nine grades heavier than the man's].[4]

A concubine in a family was treated almost as a servant except on the birth of male children and only then when the husband succeeded in avoiding the wrath of a jealous wife. Shao Fei-fei, a concubine, was remarried to a groom by a jealous wife. Since the famous statesman Chang Chien had lavished wealth and affection on his beloved concubine, Kuan P'an-p'an, she was expected to commit suicide to show her gratitude when he died. After the elapse of sufficient time in order not to embarrass his reputation, she did so.

With few exceptions over two thousand years, women held no official posts, nor were they allowed to take the examinations for entrance into the imperial bureaucracy. Other than wife, concubine or maid, a woman could be a Buddhist nun, a Taoist priestess, a courtesan, prostitute, matchmaker, herbalist or midwife. Literacy was restricted to nuns, priestesses and courtesans. However, prostitutes seem to have been prolific in writing folk songs up to modern times.

Women rarely inherited family property. According to the laws of the Ch'ing Dynasty:

The family property . . . shall be equally divided among the sons [not the daughters] no matter whether they were born to wives, concubines, or maids. The illegitimate son shall have half as much as a legitimate son . . . If the family has no sons, and no adopted son selected

4. Annotated by Ch'ang-sun Wu-chi, *T'ang Lü Shu I* (The laws of T'ang with commentaries), Taipei, 1956, vol. III, p. 98, *chüan* 22, items 9–10. According to this book the normal punishment for injuring another person with objects other than hands and feet, and causing blood to flow, is sixty lashes of a whip or stick. Therefore, if a husband injures his wife this way, he will receive from the court a sentence of forty lashes instead of sixty, and if he inflicts upon a concubine bleeding wounds, he will receive only twenty lashes.

from its clan, to inherit the property, daughters can inherit . . .[5]

The eldest son's wife who had borne a male child became matriarch after her mother-in-law's death and held absolute authority in domestic affairs. If an ambitious woman in the imperial family should become empress, she then might become *de facto* ruler. But Wu Tse-t'ien was the only empress in Chinese history to rule in her own right, after she had seized power from her husband and sons.

In India and the Far East generally, especially among the peasantry, as a woman grew older and ceased to be a sexual commodity, she gained increasing freedom and social mobility. Westerners, especially missionaries, were often shocked by the language and behavior of aged women. Partly this was due to the emergence of the ancient matriarchy as the Confucian system came to ignore the role of older women; partly, to the still surviving role of the shamaness in the folk culture; and partly to the influence of non-Chinese peoples incorporated in the empire—Tibetans, Nan-chao and Lolo, Mongols and Manchus and the people, some of them Caucasians, of the oasis cities of Central Asia. The comparative importance of upper class women under the Ch'ing Dynasty derived in part from influence of the Manchus, among whom women were more free than under the Confucian system. With the growth of Taoism as an organized religion after Han times, the Taoist high priestess took over the role of the ancient shamaness, and many of them enjoyed great influence and several were poets. Buddhist abbesses, however, seldom interfered in secular affairs.

In the anthology *Three Hundred Poems of the T'ang Dynasty*, translated by Witter Bynner under the title *The Jade Mountain*, there is only one poem written by a woman. In *Ch'üan T'ang Shih* (A Complete Collection of *Shih* Poetry of the T'ang Dynasty) among the 2200 authors, there are only around 190 women poets. In the T'ang Dynasty women were not encouraged to write poetry and very few received any literary training.

---

5. Compiled by Yao Yü-chiang, *Ta Ch'ing Lü Li Hui T'ung Hsin Tsuan* (a new, comprehensive edition of the laws and cases of the Ch'ing Dynasty), Taipei Hsien, 1964, vol. II, p. 44, *chüan* 7, "*hu la*," "*hu i*," item 14. In most cases if a family did not have male children, a boy would be selected from the members of the clan as the adopted son of the family.

Young girls in the families of the wealthier officials were sometimes allowed to study with boys in the school of their clan, or under private tutors. Daughters of great scholars or historians often became renowned scholars themselves, for instance, the poet Ts'ai Yen; but usually they were only educated enough to study books on women's conduct. Books like *Lieh Nü Chuan* (Biographies for Women), first century B.C.; *Nü Chieh* (Precepts for Women), first century A.D.; and *Kui Fan* (Standards in the Women's Quarters), sixteenth century A.D. taught women to be passive and yielding toward their husbands and parents-in-law, and modest, moderate and plain in thought, speech and appearance. For example, in *Precepts for Women*, written by the great woman historian, Pan Chao, the virtues and appearance of good women are described:

> The virtues of women are not brilliant talent, nor distinction and elegance. The virtues of women are reserve, quiet, chastity, orderliness, governing herself to maintain a sense of shame, and conducting herself according to the rules of Confucian etiquette.

> The appearance of a woman does not depend on fairness of face. The principles for a woman's appearance are to wash away dirt, wear clean and new clothing and ornaments, bathe often, and keep her body clean.[6]

In the Ch'ing (Manchu) Dynasty the ability of upper-class women to write poetry was esteemed enough to be accepted as part of a lady's dowry. A scholar-poet-official often preferred to marry an educated woman with whom he could have poetry contests, discuss the Confucian classics and the great poets. But in the same period the romantic notion that talented women were always ill-fated was a common one.[7]

Empresses and imperial concubines from noble families were often well-educated. Lower ranking women of the Imperial Palace, usually numbered in the thousands, came

6. Translated from the text quoted in Ch'en Tung-yüan, *Chung Kuo Fu Nü Shêng Huo Shih*, pp. 52–53. For an abbreviated English translation of *Nü Chieh* (Precepts for Women) by Pan Chao, see Florence Ayscough's *Chinese Women: Yesterday and Today*, Boston, 1937, pp. 237–249.

7. Ch'en Tung-yüan, pp. 191, 270.

from families of commoners, or were forfeited female relatives of officials convicted of crimes. These women sometimes became learned and were appointed by the emperor as court scholars to staff the imperial library, or as tutors to other palace women, or as monitors of the harem. The poetry of the Palace, such as that of Lady Hua Jui, generally had two subjects—praise of the emperor and of palace life, and loneliness.

According to the *Chou Li* (The Rites of the Kingdom of Chou), an emperor should have one empress and 126 concubines.[8] In reality the number of his formal consorts varied from several to more than one hundred, and the remaining palace attendants, musicians and dancers were also at his disposal. As long as they lived in the palace, many for their lifetimes, the only male they were allowed to see except eunuchs and little boys was the emperor. Since one man cannot satisfy several thousand women, these women expressed their sexual deprivation in poems of forlorn hope. According to stories, "A Poem Written on a Floating Red Leaf," attributed to a palace lady, Han Ts'ui-p'in, reached the external world by floating out in the water of the Palace garden channel.

A class of cultivated courtesans, of girls sold for reasons of poverty, or who came from disgraced official households, or were kidnapped, had flourished at least since the Six Dynasties (229–588 A.D.). They were owned by a brothel or whoremaster, and were freer than housewives and concubines. They could write love lyrics without being condemned for spoiling the family reputation. The more talented they were as poets, the more successful they were with their customers. In the Six Dynasties, China came to have something resembling a Western aristocracy, and the wealthier members kept in their palaces bands of literate women musicians and dancers called *chia chi,* "house courtesans," who entertained at banquets.

In the T'ang Dynasty (618–905 A.D.) another class of cultivated courtesans flourished, called *kuan chi,* "official courtesans," because they entertained at official festivities

8. Ibid., pp. 35–36.

and came from the most expensive brothels in the capital. Prosperous courtesans' houses were built across from the hall for imperial examinations, and when the winners were announced, the courtesans traditionally held a celebration. Leading courtiers and officials, and even the emperor, frequented these houses. When the court held great banquets these women would all be summoned. Familiar with the entire art of poetry, the most talented, such as Chao Luan-luan, would be treated as equals and join in the discussions of poetry and poetry contests that were the highlights of the banquet. Many were ransomed by wealthy, powerful men and became their concubines, among them the poet Kuan P'an-p'an. Many men poets wrote of the beauty and talent of the courtesan poets Kuan P'an-p'an, Su Hsiao-hsiao, and Hsüeh T'ao.

In the T'ang Dynasty, Taoist priestesses also became a special social class and enjoyed even more freedom than courtesans, for the priestess was no one's property. She could move, travel, and associate freely. Unlike a Buddhist nun, she was not prohibited from having intimate relations with males. Indeed, Taoist priestesses were in great demand as sexual teachers and initiators. During this period many princesses and wealthy women became priestesses and their temples became the centers of social gatherings for the scholar gentry, and they took lovers at will. The poets Yü Hsüan-chi and Li Yeh were among the most influential priestesses of their times.

The present anthology contains visionary, socialist and patriotic poetry; poems of friendship, travel and exile, as well as love lyrics. We have omitted all poems from the *Shih Ching (The Book of Songs)* for the reason that, although it is likely that many of its folk songs were composed by women, at this date authorship is difficult to determine. In the Ch'ing Dynasty most women poets repeated the themes and techniques of Li Ch'ing-chao and Chu Shu-chên, but did not excel them. Therefore we have chosen from this period Ho Shuang-ch'ing's poems on farm life and travel poems by Sun Yün-feng.

In the twentieth century, women have benefited from the loosening of the structure of traditional Chinese society and now enjoy far more education, social freedom and financial independence. Most poets, male or female, write in free verse and in the vernacular, instead of the classical forms, *shih, tz'ŭ,* and *ch'ŭ.* Since 1900 they have adapted grammar, vocabulary, technique and contents from foreign literatures. Today women poets writing in Chinese still are greatly outnumbered by men poets.[9]

LING CHUNG

---

9. *In Liu Shih Nien Tai Shih Hsüan* (Selected Poems of the 1950's), Taiwan, 1961, among twenty-six poets, two are women. In *Twentieth Century Chinese Poetry,* trans. by Kai-yü Hsü, Garden City, N.Y., 1963, there are two women among the fourty-four poets. In *Shih Hsüan, 1949–1959* (selected poems, 1949–1959), Shanghai, 1960, since no biographical information is given, I judge from names and contents of their poems that there are no women among the eighty-odd poets.

III.
Table of Chinese Historical Periods

Legendary period

The Five Emperors 3rd millennium B.C.
Hsia Dynasty c. 21st–16th century B.C.

Shang Dynasty c. 16th–11th century B.C.

Chou Dynasty 11th century–221 B.C.

Spring and Autumn period 722–481 B.C.
Warring States period 5th–3rd centuries B.C.

Ch'in Dynasty 221–206 B.C.

Han Dynasty 206 B.C.–A.D. 220

Former Han 206 B.C.–A.D. 9
Usurpation of Wang Mang A.D. 9–24
Later Han A.D. 25–220

The Three Kingdoms 220–80

The Six Dynasties 280–589

Western Chin Dynasty 265–316
Period of division between North and South 317–589

Sui Dynasty 581–617

T'ang Dynasty 618–907

The Five Dynasties 907–59

Sung Dynasty 960–1279

Northern Sung 960–1126
Southern Sung 1127–1279

Yüan (Mongol) Dynasty 1280–1367

Ming Dynasty 1368–1644

Ch'ing (Manchu) Dynasty 1644–1911

Republic of China 1912–1949

People's Republic of China 1949–

Taiwan Nationalist Government 1949–

IV.

Bibliography

This bibliography is arranged alphabetically by titles rather than by author, since the sources of the original Chinese poems have been listed by title in the notes, to facilitate comparison of texts. Most of the Chinese books listed here can be found in large university libraries in the United States. Entries for rare books include their location. A literal translation of titles is provided. In Chinese the surname precedes the given name.

Biographical Dictionary of Republican China. 4 vols. Ed. Howard L. Boorman. New York: Columbia University Press, 1967-1971.

Ch'i Shih Nien Tai Shih Hsüan (Selected Poems of the 1960's). Ed, Chang Mo and others. Kaohsiung, Taiwan: Ta Yeh Shu Tien, 1967.

Chin Yung (The Golden Pupa). Hsiung Hung. Taipei: Ch'un Wên Hsüeh Yüeh K'an Shè, 1968. Location: the Library of Congress.

Chinese Women, Yesterday and Today. Florence Ayscough. Boston: Houghton Mifflin Company, 1937.

Ch'ing Tai Fu Nü Wên Hsüeh Shih (A History of Women's Literature in the Ch'ing Dynasty). Liang I-chen. Taipei: Chung Hua Shu Chü 1958.

Ch'iu Chin Chi (A Collection of Ch'iu Chin's Writings). Ed. Chung Hua Shu Chü Shang Hai Pien Chi Shuo. Peking: Chung Hua Shu Chü, 1965.

Chiu Shih Hsin Hua (Fresh Words for Old Poems). Liu Ta-pei. Shanghai: K'ai Ming Shu Tien, 1931. Location: University of Wisconsin.

Chu Shu Chên Tuan Ch'ang Shih Tz'ŭ (The *Shih* and *Tz'ŭ* Poetry of Chu Shu-chên's *Collection of Broken Intestines).* Hongkong: Kuang Chih Shu Chü, 1960.

Ch'üan Han San Kuo Chin Nan Pei Ch'ao Shih (A Complete Collection of the *Shih* Poetry in the Han, Wei, Chin, Sung, Ch'i, Liang, Ch'en Dynasties). 6 vol. Ed. Ting Fu-pao. Taipei: I Wên Press, 1960.

Ch'üan Sung Tz'ŭ (A Complete Collection of the *Tz'ŭ* Poetry in the Sung Dynasty). 5 vols. Ed. T'ang Kuei-chang. Peking: Chung Hua Shu Chü, 1965.

Ch'üan T'ang Shih (A Complete Collection of the *Shih* Poetry in the T'ang Dynasty). 12 vols, 900 *chüan.* Ed. P'eng Ting-ch'iu and others. Peking: Chung Hua Shu Chü, 1960 (the Eighteenth Century edition).

Ch'üan Yüan San Ch'ü (A Complete Collection of the *San Ch'ü* Poetry in the Yüan Dynasty). 2 vols. Ed. Sui Shu-sên. Peking: Chung Hua Shu Chü, 1964.

Chung Hsiang Tz'ŭ (Tz'ŭ poems by the Many Fragrant). 6 vols. Ed. Hsü Shu-min and Ch'ien Yüeh. Shangheai: Ta Tung Shu Chü, 1933. Location: University of London.

Chung Hua Li Tai Fu Nü (Chinese Women of the Generations). Wang Fan-t'ing. Taipei: Commercial Press, 1966.

Chung Kuo Fu Nü (Chinese Women) Peking, 1953–1961. A monthly. Location: the Midwest Interlibrary Center.

Chung Kuo Fu Nü Shêng Huo Shih (A History of the Lives of Chinese Women). Ch'en Tung-yüan. Shanghai: Commercial Press, 1928. Location: University of Wisconsin.

Chung Kuo Fu Nü Wên Hsüeh Shih (A History of Chinese Women's Literature). Hsieh Wu-liang. Shanghai: Chung Hua Shu Chü, 1916. Location: Hoover Institute, Stanford University.

Chung Kuo Fu Nü Wên Hsüeh Shih Hua (Literary Romances of Chinese Women). Su Chih-tê. Hongkong: The Shanghai Book Co., 1963.

Chung Kuo Hsin Wên Hsüeh Ta Hsi Hsü Pien (A Supplement to Major Trends in New Chinese Literature). 10 vols. Hongkong: Hsiang Kang Wên Hsüeh Yên Chiu Shê, 1968.

Chung Kuo Nü Hsin Ti Wên Hsüeh Shêng Huo (The Literary Life of Chinese Women). T'an Chêng-pi. Shanghai: Kuang Ming Shu Chü, 1931.

Chung Kuo Wên Hsüeh Chia Ta Tz˘Tien (A Biographical Dictionary of Chinese Authors). Comp. T'an Chêng-pi. Hongkong: Wên Shih Chu Pan Shê, 1961.

Hsiao T'an Luan Shih Hui K'ê Kui Hsiu Tzŭ (Collected Tzŭ Poems of the Small Sandalwood Chamber Written by Ladies). Comp. Hsü Nai-ch'ang. (1896). Location: Harvard-Yenching Institute.

Hsing Tso (The Constellation Poetry Quarterly), no. 13 (June, 1969, published in Taiwan).

Huang Fu Jen Yüeh Fu (The Tzŭ and Ch'u Poetry of Lady Huang). Huang O. Chung Hua Shu Chü, 1940.

Ku Chin T'u Shu Chi Ch'êng (Chinese Encyclopedia) Comp. by Ch'en Mêng-lei and others. 800 vols in 86 cases. Shanghai: Chung Hua Shu Chü 1934 (1726 edition). (An index to this encyclopedia has been compiled by Lionel Giles.)

Ku Shih Hsüan (Selected Ancient Poems). Comp. Shên Tê-ch'ien. Taipei: Chung Hua Shu Chü, 1965. In the Ssŭ Pu Pei Yao Series.

Ku Shih Yüan (The Origins of Ancient Poetry). Comp. Shên Tê-ch'ien. The Ssŭ Pu Pei Yao Series.

Li Chi (The Book of Rites). 2 vols. Annot. Chêng Hsüan. The Ssŭ Pu Pei Yao Series.

Li Ch'ing-Chao Chi (A Collection of Li Ch'ing-chao's Writings). Ed. Chung Hua Shu Chü Shang Hai Pien Chi So. Peking: Chung Hua Shu Chü, 1962.

Li Tai Fu Nü Chu Tso K'ao (A Bibliography of Women's Writings over the Generations). Comp. Hu Wên-k'ai. Shanghai: Commercial Press, 1957.

Leih Nü Chuan Chiao Chu (Biographies of Women with Annotations). Taipei: Chung Hua Shu Chü, 1965. In the Ssŭ Pu Pei Yao Series.

Liu Shih Nien Tai Shih Hsüan (Selected Poems of the 1950's). Ed. Chang Mo and others. Kaohsiung, Taiwan: Ta Yeh Shu Tien, 1961.

Ming Yüan Shih Hsüan Ts'ui Lou Chi (Selected *Shih* Poems of Kingfisher Green House by Famous Ladies). Ed. Liu Yün-fên. Shanghai: Pei Yeh Shan Fang, 1936. Location: University of California, Berkeley.

Ping Hsin Shih Chi (A Collection of Ping Hsin's Poetry). Hsieh Wan-yin (Ping Hsin). Shanghai: Pei Hsin Shu Chü, 1932.

The Position of Woman in Early China According to the Lieh Nü Chuan (The Biographies of Eminent Chinese Women.) Albert Richard O'Hara. Washington, D.C.: The Catholic University of America Press, 1945.

Shih Ch'uang Tso Chi (Collected Poetry). Ed. Chung Kuo Ch'ing Nien Hsieh Tso Hsieh Hui. Taipei: Fu Hsin Shu Chü, 1965.

Sui Yüan Nü Ti Tzu Shih (The *Shih* Poetry of the Women Students of Master Sui Yüan). Ed. Yüan Mei. 1796. Location: University of California, Berkeley.

Ta Ch'ing Lü Li Hui T'ung Hsin Tsuan (A New, Comprehensive Edition of the Laws and Cases of the Ch'ing Dynasty). 5 vols. Ed. Yao Yü-hsiang. Taipei Hsien, Taiwan: Wên Hai Chu Pan Shê, 1964.

T'ang Lü Shu I (The Laws of T'ang with Commentaries). Annot. Ch'ang-sun Wu-chi. Taipei: Commercial Press, 1956.

Tz'ü Hsüeh Hsiao Ts'ung Shu (A Little Series of *Tz'ü* Poetry). Ed. Hu Yün-i. Hongkong: Chêng Fêng Shu Tien, 1953. Number 9 of this series is *Wu Tsao Tz'ü* (The *Tz'ü* Poems of Wu Tsao).

Who's Who in Communist China. Kowloon, Hongkong: Union Research Institute, 1966–to date.

Yü T'ai Hsin Yung (The New Songs of the Jade Terrace). Comp. Hsü Ling. Taipei: Chung Hua Shu Chü, 1965. The Ssŭ Pu Pei Yao Series.

Yüeh Fu Shih Chi (A Collection of *Yüeh Fu* Poetry). Comp. Kuo Mao-ch'ien. Ssŭ Pu Pei Yao Series.